P9-AQS-974

# Pennsylvania

## THE THIRTEEN COLONIES

# Pennsylvania

CRAIG A. DOHERTY

KATHERINE M. DOHERTY

Facts On File, Inc.

**Pennsylvania**

Facts On File, Inc.
132 West 31st Street
New York NY 10001

**Library of Congress Cataloging-in-Publication**

Doherty, Craig A.
    Pennsylvania / Craig A. Doherty and Katherine M. Doherty.
        p. cm. — (The thirteen colonies)
    Includes bibliographical references (p. ) and index.
    ISBN 0-8160-5413-4 (acid-free paper)
    1. Pennsylvania—History—Colonial period, ca. 1600–1775—Juvenile
literature. 2. Pennsylvania—Revolution, 1775–1783—Juvenile literature.
3. Pennsylvania—History—1775–1865—Juvenile literature.
I. Doherty, Katherine M. II. Title.
F152.D625 2005
974.8'02—dc22                      2004013403

Facts On File books are available at special discounts when purchased in bulk quantities for businesses, associations, institutions, or sales promotions. Please call our Special Sales Department in New York at (212) 967-8800 or (800) 322-8755.

You can find Facts On File on the World Wide Web at http://www.factsonfile.com.

Text design by Erika K. Arroyo
Cover design by Semadar Megged
Maps and graph by Dale Williams

Printed in the United States of America

VB FOF 10 9 8 7 6 5 4 3 2 1

This book is printed on acid-free paper.

# Note on Photos

Many of the illustrations and photographs used in this book are old, historical images. The quality of the prints is not always up to current standards, as in some cases the originals are from old or poor-quality negatives or are damaged. The content of the illustrations, however, made their inclusion important despite problems in reproduction.

# Contents

# Introduction

In the 11th century, Vikings from Scandinavia sailed to North America. They explored the Atlantic coast and set up a few small settlements. In Newfoundland and Nova Scotia, Canada, archaeologists have found traces of these settlements. No one knows for sure why the Vikings did not establish permanent colonies. It may have been that it was too far away from their homeland. At about the same time, many Scandinavians were involved with raiding and establishing settlements along the coasts of what are now Great Britain and France. This may have offered greater rewards than traveling all the way to North America.

When the western part of the Roman Empire fell in 476, Europe lapsed into a period of almost 1,000 years of war, plague, and hardship. This period of European history is often referred to as the Dark Ages or Middle Ages. Communication between the different parts of Europe was almost nonexistent. If other Europeans knew about the Vikings' explorations westward, they left no record of it. Between the time of Viking exploration and Christopher Columbus's 1492 journey, Europe underwent many changes.

By the 15th century, Europe had experienced many advances. Trade within the area and with the Far East had created prosperity for the governments and many wealthy people. The Catholic Church had become a rich and powerful institution. Although wars would be fought and governments would come and go, the countries of Western Europe had become fairly strong. During this time, Europe rediscovered many of the arts and sciences that had

Vikings explored the Atlantic coast of North America in ships similar to this one. *(National Archives of Canada)*

existed before the fall of Rome. They also learned much from their trade with the Near and Far East. Historians refer to this time as the Renaissance, which means "rebirth."

At this time, some members of the Catholic Church did not like the direction the church was heading. People such as Martin Luther and John Calvin spoke out against the church. They soon gained a number of followers who decided that they would protest and form their own churches. The members of these new churches were called Protestants. The movement to establish these new churches is called the Protestant Reformation. It had a big impact on America because many Protestant groups left Europe so they could worship the way they wanted.

In addition to religious dissent, problems arose with the overland trade routes to the Far East. The Ottoman Turks took control of the lands in the Middle East and disrupted trade. It was at this time that European explorers began trying to find a water route to the Far East. The explorers first sailed around Africa. Then an Italian named Christopher Columbus convinced the king and queen of Spain that it would be shorter to sail west to Asia rather than go around Africa. Most sailors and educated people at the time knew the world was round. However, Columbus made two errors in his calculations. First, he did not realize just how big the Earth is, and second, he did not know that the continents of North and South America blocked a westward route to Asia.

When Columbus made landfall in 1492, he believed that he was in the Indies, as the Far East was called at the time. For a period of time after Columbus, the Spanish controlled the seas and the exploration of what was called the New World. England tried to compete with the Spanish on the high seas, but their ships were no match for the floating fortresses of the Spanish Armada. These heavy ships, known as galleons, ruled the Atlantic.

In 1588, that all changed. A fleet of English ships fought a series of battles in which their smaller but faster and more maneuverable ships defeated the Spanish Armada. This opened up the New World to anyone willing to cross the ocean. Portugal, Holland, France, and England all funded voyages of exploration to the New World. In North America, the French explored the far north. The Spanish had already established colonies in what are now Florida, most of the Caribbean, and much of Central and South America. The Dutch

Depicted in this painting, Christopher Columbus completed three additional voyages to the Americas after his initial trip in search of a westward route to Asia in 1492. *(Library of Congress, Prints and Photographs Division [LC-USZ62-103980])*

bought Manhattan and established what would become New York, as well as various islands in the Caribbean and lands in South America. The English claimed most of the east coast of North America and set about creating colonies in a variety of ways.

Companies were formed in England and given royal charters to set up colonies. Some of the companies sent out military and trade expeditions to find gold and other riches. They employed men such as John Smith, Bartholomew Gosnold, and others to explore the lands they had been granted. Other companies found groups of Protestants who wanted to leave England and worked out deals that let them establish colonies. No matter what circumstances a colony was established under, the first settlers suffered hardships as

After Columbus's exploration of the Americas, the Spanish controlled the seas, largely because of their galleons, or large, heavy ships, that looked much like this model. *(Library of Congress, Prints and Photographs Division, [LC-USZ62-103297])*

**Pennsylvania**

they tried to build communities in what to them was a wilderness. They also had to deal with the people who were already there.

Native Americans lived in every corner of the Americas. There were vast and complex civilizations in Central and South America. The city that is now known as Cahokia was located along the Mississippi River in what is today Illinois and may have had as many as 50,000 residents. The people of Cahokia built huge earthen mounds that can still be seen today. There has been a lot of speculation as to the total population of Native Americans in 1492. Some have put the number as high as 40 million people.

Most of the early explorers encountered Native Americans. They often wrote descriptions of them for the people of Europe. They also kidnapped a few of these people, took them back to Europe, and put them on display. Despite the number of Native Americans, the Europeans still claimed the land as their own. European rulers and the Catholic Church at the time felt they had a right to take any lands they wanted from people who did not share their level of technology and who were not Christians.

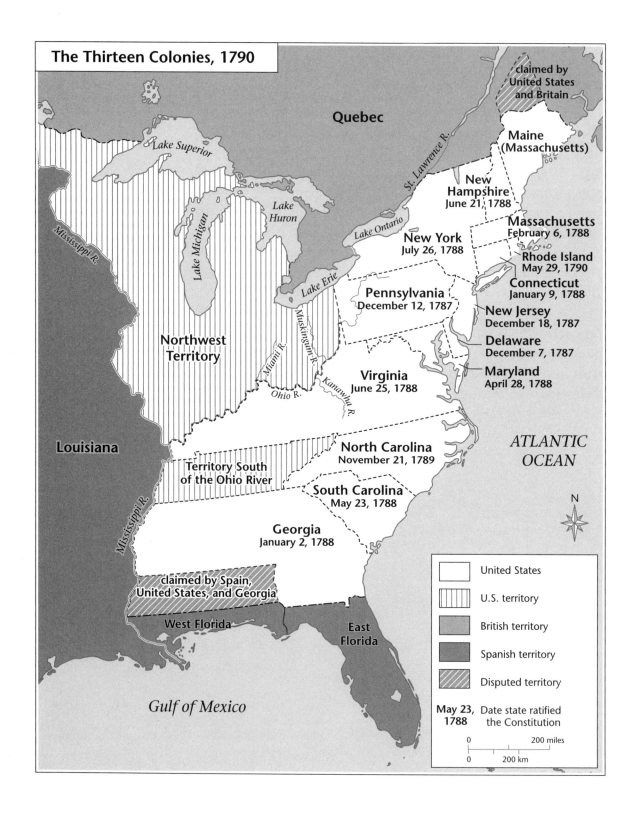

# The Thirteen Colonies, 1790

Quebec

Lake Superior

Lake Michigan

Lake Huron

Lake Ontario

Lake Erie

Mississippi R.

St. Lawrence R.

claimed by
United States
and Britain

Maine
(Massachusetts)

New
Hampshire
June 21, 1788

Massachusetts
February 6, 1788

Rhode Island
May 29, 1790

New York
July 26, 1788

Connecticut
January 9, 1788

Pennsylvania
December 12, 1787

New Jersey
December 18, 1787

Delaware
December 7, 1787

Maryland
April 28, 1788

Northwest
Territory

Miami R.

Muskingum R.

Ohio R.

Kanawha R.

Virginia
June 25, 1788

Louisiana

North Carolina
November 21, 1789

ATLANTIC
OCEAN

Territory South
of the Ohio River

South Carolina
May 23, 1788

Georgia
January 2, 1788

Mississippi R.

N

claimed by Spain,
United States, and Georgia

West Florida

East
Florida

Gulf of Mexico

United States

U.S. territory

British territory

Spanish territory

Disputed territory

May 23,
1788

Date state ratified
the Constitution

0        200 miles

0      200 km

# First Contacts

## CONFLICTING CLAIMS

The efforts to explore the Western Hemisphere that started with Christopher Columbus in 1492 increased in the late 16th and early 17th centuries. England, France, Spain, Sweden, and the Netherlands all established colonies in North America. Vast territories were claimed by the governments in Europe based on the voyages of earlier explorers. Often the lands they claimed overlapped and created conflicts that continued well after the English colonies became the United States of America.

In the area that became Pennsylvania, there were four overlapping claims based on the explorations of English explorers John Smith and Samuel Argall; Henry Hudson, an Englishman who was employed by the Dutch; and Étienne Brulé, who traveled down the Susquehanna River from the French settlement of Quebec. In addition, a group of Swedes tried to establish a trading colony in what is now Delaware and Pennsylvania.

The English established their first permanent colony in North America in 1607. It was called Jamestown and was located on

Captain John Smith helped found Jamestown in present-day Virginia. *(National Archives of Canada)*

Chesapeake Bay in what became the colony of Virginia. Captain John Smith, one of the founders of the colony, was an explorer who mapped much of the northeast coast of North America. In 1608, Smith sailed up the Susquehanna River and claimed part of what would become Pennsylvania for England.

The next claim in the area was by the Dutch. In 1609, Henry Hudson sailed west from the Netherlands in search of a shortcut to the Far East. Many people believed at the time that a passage existed that would allow ships from Europe to pass around the American continents. Hudson explored Chesapeake and Delaware Bays, where he claimed the land in the name of the Dutch. He

## Captain John Smith
### (ca. 1579–1631)

Captain John Smith helped establish the first permanent English colony in North America at Jamestown, Virginia, in 1607. Prior to that, he had been a soldier and had been captured in Hungary when fighting against the Turks. The Turks sold him into slavery but, fortunately, he was able to escape and return to England. When George Kendall, the leader of Jamestown, was charged with mutiny and shot in December 1607, Smith became the leader of the colony.

It was during this time that he made a trip to what would become Pennsylvania. In 1609, Smith was badly burned in a fire and went back to England. He returned to North America in 1614, and he made maps of most of the northeast coast. Throughout his life, he was a staunch supporter of the idea of colonizing North America. He wrote a number of books and pamphlets that

described the excellent lands that awaited anyone willing to become a colonist.

Excerpts from his books became part of advertisements that were circulated to entice people to go to North America. The following excerpt from one of Smith's books appeared in a 1636 London advertisement.

*This Country we now speak of lieth betwixt 41° and 44 1/2°, the very mean for heat and cold betwixt the Equinoctial and the North Pole, in which I have sounded about five and twenty very good harbors; in many whereof is anchorage for five hundred good ships of any burden, in some of them for a thousand: and more than three hundred isles overgrown with good timber or divers sorts of other woods; in most of them (in their seasons) plenty of wild fruits, fish, and fowl, and pure springs of most excellent water pleasantly distilling from their rocky foundations.*

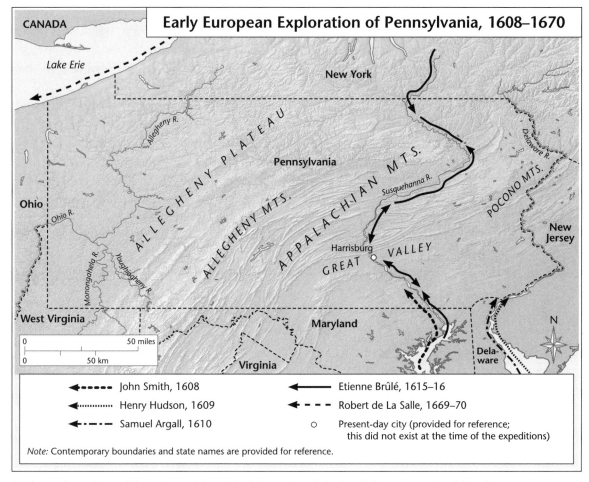

## Early European Exploration of Pennsylvania, 1608–1670

CANADA

Lake Erie

New York

Allegheny R.

ALLEGHENY PLATEAU

Pennsylvania

Ohio

Ohio R.

ALLEGHENY MTS.

APPALACHIAN MTS.

Susquehanna R.

Delaware R.

POCONO MTS.

Monongahela R.

Youghiogheny R.

Harrisburg

GREAT VALLEY

New Jersey

West Virginia

Maryland

N

Virginia

Dela-ware

0 — 50 miles
0 — 50 km

◄●●●●● John Smith, 1608

◄·········· Henry Hudson, 1609

◄–·–·– Samuel Argall, 1610

◄——— Etienne Brûlé, 1615–16

◄– – – Robert de La Salle, 1669–70

○ Present-day city (provided for reference; this did not exist at the time of the expeditions)

Note: Contemporary boundaries and state names are provided for reference.

Explorers from three different countries visited Pennsylvania before it became an English colony.

also explored the next estuary to the north, which was later named after him. The Hudson River became the center of Dutch settlement in North America. The leaders in what was called New Netherland also established trading posts on the Delaware River.

In 1610, Lord De La Warr, who had replaced Smith as governor of the Virginia colony, sent a ship north under the command of Captain Samuel Argall to explore the coast and bays. Argall sailed into a large bay that was the mouth of a substantial river. Argall named the bay and river after the governor and claimed the Delaware watershed as part of the Virginia colony.

Sponsored by the English Muscovy Company, Henry Hudson completed his first expedition in search of the Northwest Passage. *(National Archives of Canada)*

In 1608, Samuel de Champlain had established a French trading colony on the Saint Lawrence River that would grow into the city of Quebec. From this base, the French explored a vast territory. Champlain traveled into what are now New England and New York. Another French explorer, René-Robert Cavalier de La Salle, traveled throughout the region of the Great Lakes. In 1615 or 1616, Champlain sent Étienne Brulé along with some Native American guides to the headwaters of the Susquehanna River in what is now New York. Brulé and his guides paddled canoes down the river and probably reached the point where the river empties into Chesapeake Bay. Although the French were not immediately planning on settling the area that would become Pennsylvania, they were interested in trading with the Native Americans of the area. Their desire to control the fur trade in western Pennsylvania played a role in a series of

Étienne Brulé explored the Susquehanna River in the early 17th century. *(National Archives of Canada)*

wars between France and England. The four wars fought in North America from 1689 to 1763 are called the French and Indian Wars. The French armed many Native Americans who fought with them against the English.

The area that became Pennsylvania was not an empty wilderness waiting for the Europeans to come take control of it. The area was inhabited by numerous Native American groups who had lived in the area for thousands of years. It is estimated that as many as 15,000 Native Americans lived in the area that would become Pennsylvania. The Native Americans in the area were divided into two major groups based on their languages and geographical location. The largest group was called the Delaware by the Europeans. They called themselves the Lenni Lenape and lived in the eastern part of present-day Pennsylvania. They spoke a variety of Algonquian languages. To the west of the Lenni Lenape were the Susquehannock, who lived along the Susquehanna River watershed. Their languages were considered part of the Iroquoian language group. Farther to the west were a number of other tribes who were dislocated by a series of wars known as the Beaver Wars. During these wars, more powerful tribes defeated them to gain control of the area for fur trapping.

All of the Native Americans in the northeastern part of North America are referred to as Eastern Woodland Indians, and they had similar lifestyles. Sometimes they are divided into two "culture areas": Indians of the Northeast and of the Southeast. The Lenni Lenape were the most numerous of all the groups in Pennsylvania, and the way they lived was similar to all the Native American groups of the area.

The Susquehannock lived near the Susquehanna River, which flows from New York through Pennsylvania and empties into Chesapeake Bay in Maryland. This image of a Susquehannock man is a detail of a map drawn by Captain John Smith, who encountered the tribe in his travels. *(Library of Congress, Geography and Map Division)*

## THE LENNI LENAPE

When the Europeans arrived, there were approximately 40 different bands of Lenni Lenape. The name *Lenni Lenape* translates as "the original people." They lived in the Delaware River watershed, the

This image depicting a Lenni Lenape family was published in 1720 in a history of New Sweden written by Thomas Campanius Holm and known as *Campanius's*. *(University of Delaware Library)*

lower reaches of the Hudson River, and along the coastal plain of New Jersey. These people all spoke dialects of Algonquian languages and were divided by language into three distinct groups. The Lenni Lenape in the southern end of the area spoke what are called Southern Unami dialects. The people in the middle of the area spoke Northern Unami–Unalachtigo dialects. In the northern reaches of their territory, the Lenni Lenape groups spoke what are called Munsee dialects.

The Lenni Lenape belonged to the cultural group of Native Americans that anthropologists and ethnographers refer to as Northeast Woodland Indians. Like all Woodland Indians at the time, the Lenni Lenape lived in small bands that depended on farming, hunting, and fishing for their survival. A single band of the Lenni Lenape would live in three or four places during the course of the year. In the spring and the summer, they lived in an area where they planted crops. The primary crops of the Lenni Lenape were corn, beans, and a variety of squashes and gourds. Corn was the most important crop. It was the main staple of the Lenni Lenape diet and was prepared in a number of ways. Dried corn and beans were stored and eaten throughout the winter months.

The Lenni Lenape cleared their fields by burning them. When a field lost its fertility, a new area would be burned. In their fields, the Lenni Lenape made small hills of soil, in which they planted a few corn seeds each. They planted beans around the corn hills. The cornstalks served as supports for the bean vines. They planted squash between the hills to maximize the use of the cleared land.

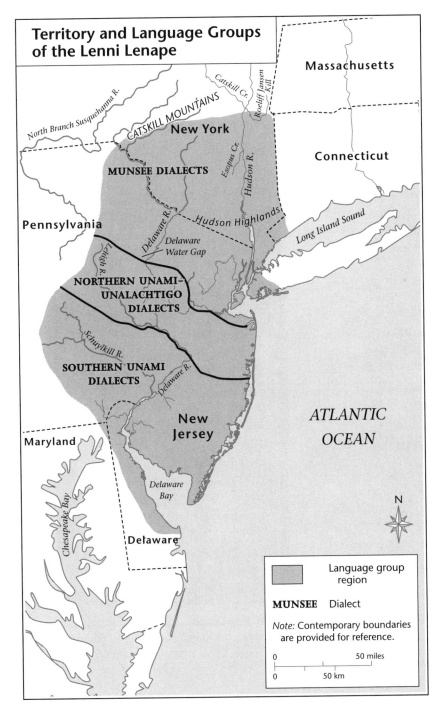

# Territory and Language Groups of the Lenni Lenape

Massachusetts

North Branch Susquehanna R.

CATSKILL MOUNTAINS

Catskill Cr.

Roeliff Jansen Kill

New York

Connecticut

**MUNSEE DIALECTS**

Esopus Cr.

Hudson R.

Pennsylvania

Delaware R.

Hudson Highlands

Long Island Sound

Delaware Water Gap

Lehigh R.

**NORTHERN UNAMI-UNALACHTIGO DIALECTS**

Schuylkill R.

**SOUTHERN UNAMI DIALECTS**

Delaware R.

New Jersey

ATLANTIC OCEAN

Maryland

Delaware Bay

Chesapeake Bay

Delaware

N

Language group region

**MUNSEE** Dialect

*Note:* Contemporary boundaries are provided for reference.

0          50 miles

0          50 km

The Lenni Lenape spoke 40 dialects of Algonquian languages and inhabited much of the eastern part of what became Pennsylvania.

In addition to food crops, the Lenni Lenape, like many other Native Americans, grew small amounts of tobacco for smoking in pipes.

The women of a band were primarily responsible for tending the crops. The Lenni Lenape men spent much of their time hunting and fishing. Fishing in the spring and summer was done in a

## Wampum

The Lenni Lenape, like many other Native American groups along the East Coast of North America, made beads using clamshells. They used a variety of clamshells to create white beads, which were always the most plentiful. They used the quahog clamshell to produce dark-colored beads that ranged in color from black to purple and blue. The beads were then strung on leather or hemp twine and fashioned into belts and jewelry.

Much of the wampum was used for decoration, but some wampum belts used a series of symbols that depicted a story or sent a message from one group to another. The Native Americans who had access to the coast often traded wampum for goods with other Native Americans in the interior of the continent. Historical accounts of contacts with the Lenni Lenape indicate that they were experts at fashioning elaborate items using wampum.

The colonists soon began to use wampum as money. In the early years of the American colonies, there was little or no money available. At first, people exchanged food as a form of currency, but this had many drawbacks—the major one being its perishable nature. If the food was not consumed, the person accepting the food would soon lose his or her profit. To solve this problem, the colonists began to accept wampum in exchange for goods, and the colonial governments set exchange rates.

Wampum's uses ranged from recording agreements to sending messages, but its use as money became more important for tribes after the arrival of European explorers and settlers. *(National Archives, Still Picture Records, NWDNS-106-IN-18A)*

variety of ways, from shore and from the canoes they made by shaping and scraping out logs. Large, weighted nets called seines, which could encircle a school of fish in shallow water; dip nets; hooks and lines; fish traps; and even bows and arrows were used to catch the abundant fish in the rivers, lakes, and bays of the Lenni Lenape territory.

The Lenni Lenape also gathered shellfish. Near the fishing camps around Delaware Bay and along the New Jersey coast, large mounds of shells accumulated. There are still remnants of these mounds at several locations in New Jersey, including near Barnegat and Tuckerton. Like many Eastern Woodland Indians, the Lenni Lenape used a variety of clamshells to create wampum for jewelry and trade.

Fish and shellfish were usually dried by laying them on racks in the sun. The dried fish were later added to soups and stews made with the corn, beans, and squash raised in the fields. In addition to fish and shellfish, the Lenni Lenape hunted and ate all sorts of wild game. Deer was the most important game they pursued, and all parts of the animal were used in some way. The meat was eaten fresh as well as dried. The hide was used to make clothes. The bones and antlers were made into a wide variety of tools. The sinew, which connects the muscles to the bone, was used like string.

Large groups of Lenni Lenape worked together to drive deer into large traps where they could be more easily harvested. During these deer drives, the Lenni Lenape often used fire to force the deer in an area toward their traps. These communal hunts required the cooperation of several bands of Lenni Lenape. In addition to deer, the Lenni Lenape harvested many other animals.

Moose, bear, and many small animals and birds were hunted or trapped. In the spring, many Lenni Lenape traveled to areas where

This engraving by Theodor de Bry, based on a painting by John White, records the Algonquian village of Secotan, including residents' homes and some corn crops. *(Library of Congress, Prints and Photographs Division [LC-USZ62-52444])*

## Corn

Corn, known as maize, was first domesticated 6,000 to 8,000 years ago in Central America. Its cultivation spread until it was grown throughout the temperate regions of North America. Corn is a member of the grass family. Through careful seed selection and hybridization, Native Americans were able to develop many varieties of corn and adapt its growth to a wide range of climatic zones. In Pennsylvania, the Native Americans grew three main varieties of corn. The most important type was dried and ground into cornmeal to make a variety of dishes. They also grew a variety of corn that was dried whole and added to soups and stews throughout the winter. It was also eaten fresh, like modern corn on the cob. They also cultivated a type of corn that was used as popcorn.

the now-extinct passenger pigeon nested to gather the young birds called squab from the nest. Turkeys were also plentiful in the area of the Lenni Lenape. They ate turkeys and used the feathers as decoration for their clothing and headdresses.

The Lenni Lenape had two similar types of shelters. At their hunting, fishing, and farming locations, they often built small huts known as wigwams by placing the ends of saplings (young, flexible trees) in the ground in a circle. They then bent the tops of the saplings into the middle to form a dome. The dome was covered with bark. The floors were covered with woven reed mats. In the winter, the Lenni Lenape usually lived in more permanent villages.

The winter villages were often built on the top of a hill and were surrounded by a stockade or palisade made of logs. Inside the stockade, there would be a number of "long-houses." A longhouse was also built using saplings, but instead of setting them in a circle, the Lenni Lenape would arrange saplings in two long rows. The tops of the saplings were then tied together to form a long, arched frame. The frame was covered with

Native Americans used almost every part of the white-tailed deer that they killed. *(National Park Service)*

In this illustration published in a 1702 history of New Sweden, some Lenni Lenape longhouses are surrounded by a stockade, or a perimeter made of tall timbers sharpened at one end and driven into the ground. *(University of Delaware Library)*

large sections of chestnut tree bark that were often six feet long. The largest longhouses were more than 100 feet long and 20 feet wide. A longhouse of this size was divided into family sections, and as many as seven to 10 families lived in it. A slot was left open along the peak of the roof of the longhouse to allow smoke from the cooking fires to escape.

Throughout the winter, the families in a longhouse prepared their meals in large clay pots, and they primarily ate soups and stews. The floors of the longhouse were covered with woven mats. Similarly decorated mats covered the walls. Their beds were made from the hides of animals with the fur left on for comfort and warmth. The family sections of the longhouse were divided by partitions, and each family had its own cooking fire. Among the Lenni Lenape, as with many Native American groups, there was very little in the way of private property, and the survival of the band depended on the cooperation of the group.

When Europeans first arrived in New Netherland, New Sweden, and eventually Pennsylvania, the Lenni Lenape were eager to trade with them for metal goods, cloth, and other manufactured items that they did not have. The Europeans wanted to get the pelts of various animals, especially beaver, which were in high demand in Europe. As the colonists spread out, they adopted many Lenni Lenape names for places and geographical features of areas that are still used today.

William Penn, the founder of Pennsylvania, treated the Lenni Lenape and other Native American groups better than other European leaders did. However, the Lenni Lenape suffered from exposure to European diseases that were previously unknown in North America and to which they had no immunity. Diseases such as chicken pox, measles, and smallpox killed many more Lenni Lenape than did direct conflicts with the colonists. As more and more colonists flooded into the Lenni Lenape territory, armed conflicts arose with the Dutch in the eastern areas. Eventually, those Lenni Lenape who survived the fighting and European diseases migrated westward. The remaining Lenni Lenape ended up on reservations, or lands reserved for a tribe by the federal government, in the Midwest and West. Today, there is an active group of Native Americans in Oklahoma who consider themselves the descendants of the Pennsylvania Lenni Lenape.

# 2

# First Settlements in Pennsylvania

## THE DUTCH

In 1624, the Dutch established the colony of New Netherland on Manhattan Island. Their first settlement was called New Amsterdam. It later became New York. The main purpose of the colony was to promote the fur trade with the Native Americans throughout the Hudson River watershed. In addition to settlements at New

This detail of a 17th-century map of New Netherland by Nicolaes Visscher is a vignette of New Amsterdam, which would later become New York City. *(Library of Congress)*

Amsterdam and Albany, which the Dutch called Beverwyck (Beavertown), they established a trading post called Fort Casimir on the eastern shore of the Delaware River. Although they technically did not settle on the lands that are now Pennsylvania, these early Dutch settlers traded with the Lenni Lenape on both sides of the river and most likely visited the Pennsylvania side of the river on a number of occasions.

Peter Minuit, who had been the governor of the Dutch colony, was fired by the Dutch West India Company, the organization in charge of New Netherland, and returned to Europe in 1631. Minuit believed there was still money to be made in the fur trade,

## Peter Minuit
### (1580–1638)

Peter Minuit is remembered by historians for his role in establishing the Dutch colony on Manhattan Island. It is reported that he exchanged approximately 60 guilders' ($24) worth of trade goods with a group of Native Americans for the island. Most likely the Native Americans assumed that the Dutch were just paying to use their land, as they did not have the same ideas about property ownership that the Europeans had. After leading the Swedish settlers to the west bank of the Delaware River, Minuit died at sea during a hurricane on his trip back to Europe in 1638.

The legends of the Dutch purchase of Manhattan and Staten Islands, such as that of Peter Minuit (shown here) buying Manhattan Island for 60 guilders, illustrates the difference between the Native Americans' and the colonists' understanding of ownership and land. *(Library of Congress)*

and he went to Sweden where he convinced Queen Christiana to back an attempt to establish a Swedish colony.

## NEW SWEDEN

With Minuit as their guide, in 1638 a small group of Swedish settlers and soldiers arrived in Delaware Bay, selected a spot on the west side of the bay, and built a fort. They named it Fort Christiana after the queen of Sweden. The location of the fort later became the site of Wilmington, Delaware. After getting the colonists settled, Minuit left New Sweden to return to Europe.

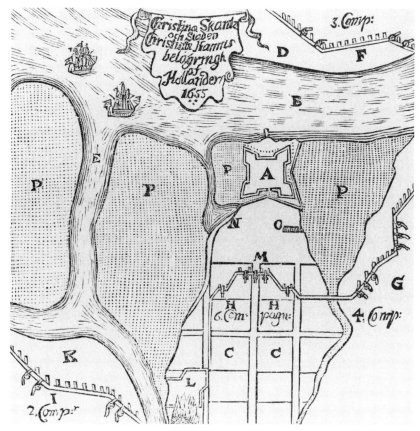

A diagram of Fort Christiana published in *Campanius's* (an early 18th-century history of New Sweden), shows its location on the Christina River in Delaware Bay (present-day Wilmington, Delaware). *(Delaware Public Archives, Dover, Delaware)*

Peter Stuyvesant became director of New Netherland in 1647. *(Delaware Public Archives, Dover, Delaware)*

In 1643, Queen Christiana sent Johan Printz to New Sweden to serve as governor. Printz did not like Fort Christiana's location because he felt it would be hard to defend if it was attacked. Printz decided to move the capital farther up the bay to Tinicum Island. Twenty miles south of what is now Philadelphia, it became the first European settlement in Pennsylvania. The Swedes called it New Gothenburg after a city in Sweden.

By this time, a number of Swedes had arrived in New Sweden. Although New Sweden did not last long as a colony, the settlers there made a lasting contribution to the American experience: the log cabin. Their unique style of building houses became that of the house of choice throughout the American frontier well into the 19th century. Trees were plentiful, and all a settler needed was an ax to build a cabin.

New Sweden remained one of the smallest colonies in North America. The land the Swedes settled was claimed by both the Dutch and the English. Sweden was a prosperous country at the time and very few people wanted to leave and settle in North America. Relations between New Sweden and New Netherland became more and more strained as time went on. Both colonies tried to control the trade with the Lenni Lenape who lived along the Delaware River watershed.

In 1653, Johan Rising, Johan Printz's successor as governor, attacked and captured Fort Casimir, a Dutch settlement on the Delaware. Peter Stuyvesant, the Dutch governor, was extremely upset and began harassing the Swedish settlements. In 1655, Stuyvesant headed a military expedition from New Amsterdam to the Delaware River. He had seven ships and more than 300 soldiers under his command.

Confronted by a force that was almost as big as the entire population of New Sweden, Governor Rising had no choice but to surrender. New Sweden ceased to exist, and the Swedish settlers were

# Johan Printz
## (1592–1663)

Johan Printz was the governor of New Sweden for 10 years (1643–53). During that time the colony expanded to about 500 settlers and was constantly at peril from the Dutch to the north and east, and from the English to the south. The Lenni Lenape called Printz "Big Belly." He is reported to have been almost seven feet tall and weighed close to 400 pounds.

allowed to stay as long as they swore allegiance to the Dutch. The Dutch held onto the settlements in what would become Delaware, New Jersey, and Pennsylvania for less than 10 years before they, too, lost their colony.

Photographed in 1940, this log cabin in the vicinity of present-day Darby, Pennsylvania, was built between 1640 and 1650. *(Library of Congress, Prints and Photographs Division [HABS, PA, 23-DARB.V, 2-1])*

## ENGLISH CONQUEST

In the middle of the 17th century, there were numerous problems in England. King Charles I was overthrown by the Puritans, who were led by Oliver Cromwell. Cromwell and his Puritan followers ruled England for 10 years until the monarchy was restored in 1660. At that time, Charles I's son, Charles II, returned from exile and became the king of England.

As king, Charles II had many supporters he wanted to reward. One of them was his brother James. One of the ways Charles II rewarded his brother was to give him a large tract of land in North America. The only problem was that James's lands were the same lands claimed by the Dutch in New Netherland.

Colonel Richard Nicolls commanded a fleet of English ships that arrived at New Amsterdam in September 1664 and captured the colony without firing a shot. New Netherland became New York. Shortly after, James designated the lands between the Hudson and Delaware Rivers as the colony of New Jersey. The land west of the Delaware River was left in a state of limbo for almost 20 years until it was granted to William Penn on March 4, 1681.

Charles II ruled England, Scotland, and Ireland from 1660 until his death in 1685. *(Library of Congress, Prints and Photographs Division [LC-USZ62-96910])*

Peter Stuyvesant governed the Dutch colony of New Amsterdam (later New York City) until his surrender on September 8, 1664, to an English force led by Colonel Richard Nicolls. *(Library of Congress, Prints and Photographs Division [LC-USZ62-84401])*

## THE CREATION OF PENNSYLVANIA

Pennsylvania was created as a "holy experiment" by the Quaker William Penn (1644–1718). How one man came to be responsible for establishing one of the original thirteen colonies is an important story. William Penn was born into the privileged upper class in England. His father, who was also named William Penn, was a successful naval officer who owned estates in England and Ireland. The younger Penn was brought up with all the privileges of his class. He was educated by private tutors and attended the best schools.

However, Penn did not follow in his father's footsteps. While visiting the family estates in Ireland, the younger Penn heard Thomas Loe talk about being a Quaker and the beliefs of the Quaker religious group. It seems that Penn was very interested. While attending Oxford University, Penn began his religious dissent by refusing to attend the official Anglican Church services of the college. In his second year at Oxford, he was expelled for his actions.

## James, Duke of York and Albany, Later King James II
### (1633–1701)

In 1649, King Charles I was removed from the throne and executed after a Puritan revolution in England. His two sons, Charles, prince of Wales, and James, duke of York and Albany, were forced to spend the next eight years living in exile while the Puritan Oliver Cromwell ran England. Charles lived in poverty in the Netherlands, and James went to Spain, where he joined the Spanish navy in its war against Protestant England. When the English monarchy was restored in 1660, James's older brother became Charles II, king of England.

Charles II appointed James lord high admiral of the navy, and in 1664, granted James all the lands between the Connecticut and Delaware Rivers in North America. James sent a fleet to capture the territory claimed by the Dutch and was involved with the fate of New York and New Jersey for the next 24 years.

In 1672, James created a controversy by revealing that he had converted to Catholicism. Although England tolerated many different Protestant sects, the country was not tolerant of Catholics. In fact, in 1673, Parliament passed the Test Act, a law that barred Catholics from holding office. James was forced to resign his position as lord high admiral.

Because his brother had not produced an heir, James was next in line to become king of England. On his brother's death in 1685, many tried to block James from becoming king. They were unsuccessful, and he became James II, king of England.

As king, he was faced with a number of uprisings in England. He was extremely brutal in addressing any resistance to his rule. He was so unpopular that, in 1688, he was removed from the throne in a bloodless coup, or overthrow, known as the Glorious Revolution. After a brief and unsuccessful attempt to regain his throne, he spent the rest of his life in exile in France.

## The Quakers

During the 17th century, a number of new Protestant sects developed in opposition to the official Anglican Church in England. The government often persecuted these groups, and in 1649, the Puritans overthrew the government of King Charles I primarily in an effort to impose their religious beliefs on the country.

In 1647, George Fox (1624–91) began preaching a new way of looking at religion. He said that all people were equal in the eyes of God and that they did not need ministers and fancy churches to find salvation. He believed that all people had an "inner light" that was their direct guidance from God. He and his followers claimed that just before they came in touch with this inner light, their bodies would quake uncontrollably.

In 1650, after spending a year in prison, Fox was brought to court for preaching his beliefs. In court he told the judge that he should "tremble at the word of the Lord." The judge was not impressed with Fox's warning and referred to Fox and his followers as "quakers." Despite the persecution Fox and his followers experienced, the group grew rapidly. They believed that all people were equal in the eyes of God, and they refused to show respect for the upper classes and other authorities in England. They also were pacifists (against war) and refused to join the military. At this time, England was almost constantly at war, and the pacifist teachings of the Quakers were seen as unpatriotic.

The English authorities persecuted the Quakers more than any other religious group. At one point, more than 4,000 Quakers were in jail, and over the years more than 15,000 Quakers were imprisoned in England. Even in the colonies,

The senior Penn sent his son on a tour of Europe in the hope that he might outgrow his religious rebellion. Then, to try and keep him out of trouble, his father sent Penn back to Ireland, where he once again met Thomas Loe. It was at this point, in 1662, that William Penn decided to become a Quaker. He returned to England committed to work on behalf of his beliefs.

In part because of his education and position in society, William Penn quickly became one of the leaders of the Quakers. He wrote extensively about their beliefs and was imprisoned at least four times. He could easily have used his family connections to avoid prison but did not. The senior Penn had been a staunch supporter of Charles II and had loaned him large sums of money

Quakers were not welcome. Some Quakers who refused to follow the Puritan rules of the Massachusetts colony were executed. Leaders of the movement, including Fox, were in and out of prison on a regular basis.

Despite this, the number of Quakers grew rapidly, and it is estimated that by 1680 there may have been as many as 60,000 Quakers in England. By this time, the group had become organized and adopted the name "Society of Friends." Their churches were simple meetinghouses, and they employed no ministers. On Sundays, Quakers would go to meetinghouses and sit quietly. If people in the group wished to share their prayers or thoughts they could do so, but there was no organized service. The majority of the Quakers came from the middle classes, and when they began to move to Pennsylvania people from all walks of life added to the energy that created one of the most prosperous colonies in the Americas.

George Fox founded the Society of Friends, or Quakers. *(Library of Congress, Prints and Photographs Division [LC-USZ62-5790])*

to help reestablish the monarchy. When the senior Penn died, the debt was owed to his son, who inherited his father's estates.

With his newfound wealth, William Penn first tried to get involved in West New Jersey, where a number of Quakers had moved to find a place where they would not be persecuted. For a number of reasons, the situation in West New Jersey did not work out, and Penn realized the only way he could create a haven for Quakers in America was to start his own colony. At this point, he proposed to Charles II that instead of paying the debt owed to his father's estate, he be given land in America.

After a period of negotiations that involved the king's brother James, who had earlier been given the land, it was agreed that

In 1681, Charles II granted a tract of land to William Penn, whose portrait is shown here, to honor Penn's father. *(Library of Congress, Prints and Photographs Division [LC-USZ62-106735])*

William Penn would receive a large grant of land west of the Delaware River, bounded by Maryland on the south and New York on the north. There was a certain amount of debate over the name of the new colony. Penn wanted to call it New Wales, because its green rolling hills reminded him of Wales, part of Britain. Some Welsh people in the government objected. Penn then suggested that it be called Sylvania, which means "land of woods." Charles II wanted to honor Penn's father and suggested that Pennsylvania would be more acceptable to him.

With the granting of a charter in 1681, the colony of Pennsylvania was created with William Penn as the sole proprietor. As proprietor, Penn was granted full control of the colony as long as he did not go against the existing laws that governed English people. Penn saw his colony as a "holy experiment" and set about creating a place that gave colonists more freedom and more rights than in any of the existing colonies.

## The Land Granted to William Penn in the Charter of Pennsylvania

*Doe give and Grant unto the said William Penn, his Heires and Assignes, all that Tract or Parte of Land in America, with all the Islands therein conteyned, as the same is bounded on the East by Delaware River, from twelve miles distance Northwards of New Castle Towne unto the three and fortieth degree of Northerne Latitude, if the said River doeth extende so farre Northwards; But if the said River shall not extend soe farre Northward, then by the said River soe farr as it doth extend; and from the head of the said River, the Easterne Bounds are to bee determined by a Meridian Line, to bee drawne from the head of the said River, unto the said three and fortieth Degree. The said Lands to extend westwards five degrees in longitude, to bee computed from the said Easterne Bounds; and the said Lands to bee bounded on the North by the beginning of the three and fortieth degree of Northern Latitude and on the South by a Circle drawne at twelve miles distance from New Castle Northward and Westward unto the beginning of the fortieth degree of Northern Latitude, and then by a straight Line Westward to the Limit of Longitude above-mentioned.*

To make sure the Quakers and others would have the freedom that Penn believed God had granted them, Penn drew up a set of rules to govern the colony. This document is called the First Frame of Government. In the First Frame of Government, Penn outlined how his colony would be organized. He was to be governor and willingly share power with an elected council of 72 and an elected assembly of 200 members

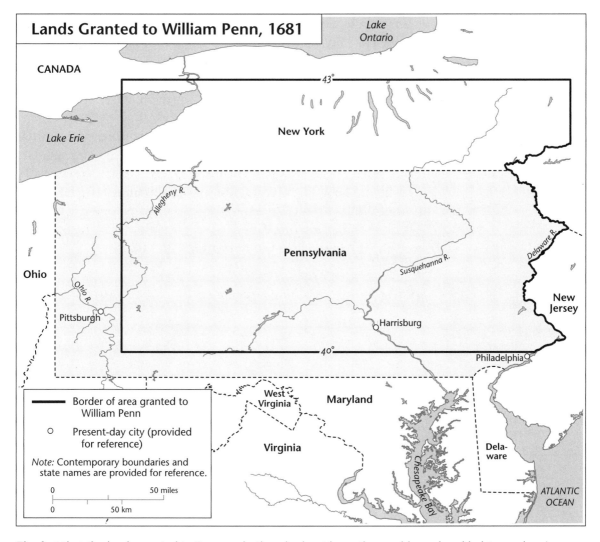

**Lands Granted to William Penn, 1681**

- Border of area granted to William Penn
- ○ Present-day city (provided for reference)

*Note:* Contemporary boundaries and state names are provided for reference.

0 — 50 miles
0 — 50 km

The fact that the lands granted to Penn and others had not been thoroughly explored led to overlapping claims and later conflicts.

Under the First Frame of Government, Pennsylvania had more liberal rules for allowing people to vote than in any other colony. About half the people in Pennsylvania were allowed to vote. In other colonies, only about a quarter of the people qualified to participate in elections. In part because of the way he had been treated by the courts in England, Penn made sure that Pennsylvania would have a fair and impartial court system in which individuals had the right to have jury trials.

Penn also made his colony different in another way. Penn believed the Native Americans in Pennsylvania were his equals in the eyes of God. Therefore, they were to be treated the same as any other people in the colony. The Native Americans were also provided the same rights under the laws, and their lands could not be taken without payment as was the norm in most of the other colonies.

What Penn tried to create was in many ways the model that the Patriots would follow when it came time to declare independence from Britain and set up the United States. Liberty, justice, and equality for all got its first real test in Pennsylvania under the direction of William Penn. The rapid growth of the colony and its success is an indication that Penn was on the right track when it came to truly providing a land of opportunity for all.

# 3

# The Quakers
# in Pennsylvania

Unlike some of the colonies that had taken many years to attract settlers, Pennsylvania was an almost instant success. By 1685, more than 8,000 people had moved to the colony. The first waves of settlers were Quakers from England, Wales, and Ireland. Penn came to his colony in 1682 on the ship *Welcome*. Despite Penn's careful planning, settlers often faced the hardships of traveling to and settling in a new land.

On the *Welcome*, smallpox ravaged the crew and colonists. William Penn had survived smallpox as a child. This gave him immunity to the disease, and he spent his time on the voyage tending the sick. Thirty people on the ship died. When the *Welcome* reached Delaware Bay, Penn's first stop was at New Castle, Delaware. This tiny remnant of New Sweden had been given to Penn by James, duke of York and Albany, and was called the "lower counties" while it was part of Pennsylvania. In 1701, Penn allowed the lower counties to have their own assembly, but the Penns remained the proprietors until the American Revolution.

After stopping at New Castle, Penn continued 20 miles up the Delaware River, where he and the colonists traveling with him set up their first community and the temporary capital of the colony. It is reported that Penn turned to one of his fellow travelers and asked what they should name their new town. The colonist suggested Chester after his hometown in England. Penn agreed, and Chester, Pennsylvania, became the first official colony in

Built in 1721 and photographed in 1958, this gristmill, used to grind grain, in Chester County, Pennsylvania, has operated continuously since its construction. *(Library of Congress, Prints and Photographs Division [HABS, PA, 15-SCON.V, 1-1])*

Pennsylvania. However, Penn had bigger plans for the permanent capital of his colony.

## PHILADELPHIA

Like many educated men of his time, Penn's interests were widespread. When it came time to lay out the main community of the colony, Penn was actively involved. Many of the cities in Europe had grown in a haphazard fashion and were overcrowded. In 1666, a large portion of London had burned and those who were charged with rebuilding it used the opportunity to apply new ideas in city planning. Streets were straightened and widened to make it possible for future fires to be more easily contained.

Penn wanted his capital to be a "green country town" with wide streets, large lots, and open areas. He decided to call the place

Philadelphia, which means "brotherly love" in Greek. The site that his surveyor, the Irishman Thomas Holme, selected was called Coaquannock by the Lenni Lenape, which translates as "grove of pines." Holme and Penn's cousin, William Markham, who was Penn's deputy governor, arrived in the colony in 1681. They started laying out the town, using a rectangular grid with the Delaware River as one boundary and the Schuylkill River as the other. In Quaker fashion, the streets were given plain names such as Chestnut, Front, Broad, and Walnut.

Originally, Holme had planned to give out the building sites in the city via a lottery. However, Penn arrived before he did that and assigned the lots himself. This caused some controversy because Penn gave the best lots to those who had invested in the colony or had already purchased large tracts from the proprietor. Although this seemed to go against Penn's ideas of equality for all, it was no doubt a practical business necessity. It seemed only natural that a

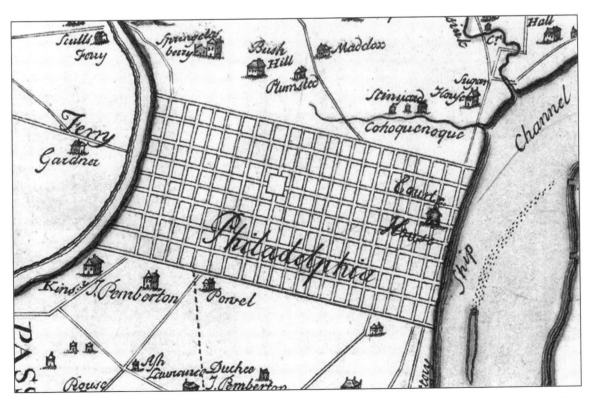

Philadelphia's city streets, neatly laid out between the Delaware and Schuylkill Rivers, are clear in this detail of a 1752 map by Nicholas Scull. *(Library of Congress)*

## Brick by Brick

The first houses in Philadelphia were most likely built with wood from the trees that were cut as the land was cleared for the city. However, people soon discovered that the banks of the local rivers and streams contained deposits of clay that was suitable for making bricks. By the middle of the 18th century, the vast majority of the buildings in Philadelphia were built using red bricks. From the huge mansions of the colony's richest merchants and landowners down to compact row houses, bricks became the building material of choice. Brick buildings presented a number of advantages. First, they were almost fire-proof. They also required little maintenance to look good. A brick house was also easier to heat in the winter and remained cooler in the summer. They also made Philadelphia quickly look like a city of substance that had been rooted to its spot for a while.

Photographed in the 1930s, this brick merchant's house in Philadelphia was built between 1703 and 1715. *(Library of Congress, Prints and Photographs Division [HABS, PA, 51-PHILA, 45-1])*

group such as the Free Society of Traders have almost 100 acres along the harbor. The group purchased 20,000 acres from Penn, with the intention of becoming one of the colony's economic leaders.

The work on Philadelphia progressed rapidly. By 1683, there were already 100 houses and 600 people living there. Two years later, in 1685, 2,500 people were there. Some were even living in caves dug into the banks of the Delaware River as they waited for their houses to be completed. While some colonies suffered because they could not attract enough new colonists, Pennsylvania grew rapidly. By 1710, Philadelphia was one of the largest cities in North America. Thanks to Penn's planning, many considered it the most beautiful city as well.

## PENN AND THE INDIANS

In 1682, William Penn wanted to make good on his promise to treat the Native Americans of Pennsylvania as equals. A meeting was called with the leaders of the Lenni Lenape, the Susquehannock, and some other smaller tribes. The chief of the Lenni Lenape, Tamanend, presented Penn with a wampum belt to commemorate the meeting. It depicts an Indian and a Quaker shaking hands in friendship.

The agreement that Penn negotiated with the chiefs is referred to as the "Great Treaty" and was respected for many years by both sides. When the first of a series of wars between the English colonists and the French and their Indian allies to the north took place, Pennsylvania remained a place of peace between the two groups. Even later, when greed overcame settlers and they violated the Great Treaty, the Indians continued to respect it. It was not until the fourth and final war, known as the French and Indian War (1755–62) that serious fighting took place in Pennsylvania.

The Native Americans in Pennsylvania did slowly leave as they sold their rights to more and more land in the colony. As white

### An Excerpt from William Penn's Address to the Chiefs

When Penn met with the chiefs just north of Philadelphia toward the end of 1682, he is reported to have said,

*The Great Spirit who made me and you, who rules the heavens and the Earth, and who knows the innermost thoughts of men, knows that I and my friends have a hearty desire to live in peace and friendship with you.*

*The Great God who is the power and wisdom that made you and me Incline your hearts to Rightousness Love and peace. This I send to Assure you of my Love, and to desire your Love to my friends, and when the Great God brings me among you I Intend to order all things in such manner that we may all live in Love and peace one with another which I hope the Great God will Incline both me and you to do. I seek nothing but the honor of his name, and that we who are his workmanship, may do that which is well pleasing to him. The man which delivers this into you, is my Special friend Sober wise and Loving, you may believe him. I have already taken care that none of my people wrong you, by good Laws I have provided for that purpose, nor will I ever allow any of my people to sell Rumme to make your people drunk. If anything should be out of order, expect when I come, it shall be mended, and I will bring you some things of our Country that are useful and pleasing to you. So I rest In ye Love of our god yt made us I am*

England 21 : 2 : 1682

your Loveing Freind

WM PENN.

I sent this to the Indians
by an Jntr.pr. ye
6 mo 1682 Tho. Holme

After receiving a charter from King Charles, William Penn informed Native Americans inhabiting the area that would become Pennsylvania of his intentions to establish an English colony there and negotiated this treaty with them. *(Library of Congress, Prints and Photographs Division [LC-USZ62-3933])*

settlers pushed ever westward, the remaining Native Americans moved ahead of them. Some continued west, like the Lenni Lenape who eventually ended up in the Indian Territories (Oklahoma). Others went north, settling in Canada.

## INDUSTRY AND AGRICULTURE

William Penn pointed out in one of his pamphlets promoting Pennsylvania that it was situated 600 miles south of London's latitude. The climate in the colony was ideal in many respects. Pennsylvanians escaped the harsh winters that those in New England often suffered through. During the summers, on the other hand, Pennsylvanians often did not experience the overwhelming heat that those in the Deep South had to endure. Like the Quakers who settled there, the climate of Pennsylvania was the perfect example of moderation.

Adequate rainfall, rich soil, and a long growing season soon made Pennsylvania the breadbasket of the colonies. Even today, agriculture is extremely important to the state and many crops were and are grown there. The first settlers in Pennsylvania grew wheat and other grains. They also adopted Native American crops such as corn and tobacco, which became a valuable cash crop for the farmers of the colony. In addition, many settlers in Pennsylvania grew flax. The fibers of the flax plant were spun into thread and then woven into cloth known as linen.

Livestock also proliferated in Pennsylvania. Horses, cows, chickens, pigs, and other European farm animals arrived with the settlers in the colony. In addition to domestic livestock, the woods of Pennsylvania teemed with wildlife. Elk, deer, bear, turkeys, and numerous small game birds and animals

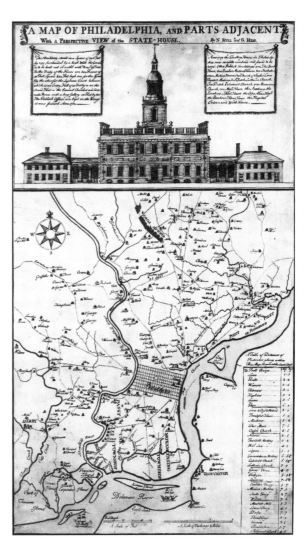

This image of Philadelphia and its State House is a detail of a map drawn by Nicholas Scull and George Heap and published in 1752, near the end of the State House's 23-year construction period. The building later served as the location of the 1787 constitutional convention. *(Library of Congress)*

# The Pennsylvania Rifle

Most of the guns the English brought with them to the Americas were smoothbore muskets that were not very accurate. Starting sometime in the middle of the 16th century, Swiss gunmakers invented the technique of putting twisting grooves in the barrel. These grooves (known as "rifling") caused the bullet to spin when it was fired. The spinning bullet traveled much straighter and farther than a similar bullet fired from a smoothbore. In the early days of the Pennsylvania colony, Swiss and German gunmakers settled in Lancaster County and began making rifles. Their original rifles were heavy and fired a very-large-caliber ball. They soon adapted their designs to the needs of Pennsylvania woodsmen. Lighter rifles that fired a .40 to .50 caliber ball through a longer barrel became the weapon known throughout the colonies as the Pennsylvania rifle. They were accurate to 300 yards and gave American soldiers an advantage in the Revolutionary War.

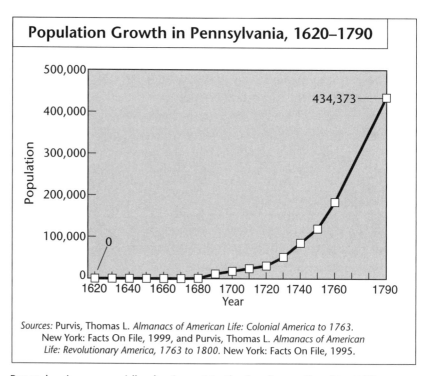

**Population Growth in Pennsylvania, 1620–1790**

Sources: Purvis, Thomas L. *Almanacs of American Life: Colonial America to 1763.* New York: Facts On File, 1999, and Purvis, Thomas L. *Almanacs of American Life: Revolutionary America, 1763 to 1800.* New York: Facts On File, 1995.

Pennsylvania grew rapidly, due in part to the freedoms offered by William Penn and the suitability of the land and climate.

found their way onto the tables in Pennsylvania. The hunters of the colony had the added advantage of the Pennsylvania rifle. The colony was soon exporting the excess produce of its farms to markets throughout the world.

The port of Philadelphia quickly became one of the busiest in the colonies. To meet the needs of the growing commerce of the colony, shipbuilding became an important industry in Philadelphia. Other industries and crafts flourished in the colony as well. Because many Quakers came from the artisan class in Britain, the colony soon was making many items that other colonies had to import. Metalworkers, carriage makers, furniture makers, glass makers, and many others hung their signs on the streets of Philadelphia. Sawmills and gristmills sprang up throughout the colony to process the bountiful harvest from forests and fields.

The colony of Pennsylvania offered opportunities for people from all walks of life who wanted to benefit from the guarantees of freedom promised and delivered by William Penn. Business and agriculture flourished, and the population grew rapidly. However,

## Paper and Printing Presses

In 1682, William Bradford (1663–1752), an English Quaker, arrived in Philadelphia. He soon set up the first printing press in the colony. However, he constantly faced the problem of finding and purchasing imported paper, which was very expensive. To solve that problem, he partnered with William Rittenhouse and others to set up the first paper mill in America. In 1690, using water power from the Schuylkill River, they began making paper using scraps of cloth. It was not until the 19th century that people began making paper using wood fibers. Today, 95 percent of all paper is made from wood fiber.

Bradford ended up being forced to leave Pennsylvania for printing the works of the Scottish minister George Keith. Individuals in Pennsylvania were allowed complete freedom of religion, but this freedom apparently did not extend to those who wished to publish material that the leaders of the colony considered "seditious libel." Bradford moved to New York, where he became the official printer for that colony. Rittenhouse continued in the paper business, and in 1719, Bradford's son Andrew published the *American Weekly Mercury,* Pennsylvania's first newspaper.

William Penn was forced to return to London to deal with a serious problem that faced the colony.

## PROBLEMS FOR PENN AND HIS COLONY

Fifty years before William Penn received his charter for Pennsylvania, George Calvert, Lord Baltimore, had convinced Charles I to grant him a large tract of land north of the Potomac River in what was at the time the colony of Virginia. Lord Baltimore had recently admitted to being a Catholic and wanted to create a colony in North America where members of his faith could go and live without fear of being persecuted by the Protestant majority in England.

Baltimore called his colony Maryland, and because those who drew up his land grant, and later Penn's, were unfamiliar with the actual lands they were describing, Maryland claimed much of the southern part of the land granted to William Penn. It soon became apparent that Penn would have to return to London to try to resolve the dispute with his southern neighbors. In fact, it was not until the 1760s that the boundary between Maryland and Pennsylvania was finally settled.

On his return to London, Penn was received cordially by Charles II. However, the king who had granted him Pennsylvania was in poor health, and no resolution to the boundary problem came about. Charles II died in 1685 without any children to succeed him, so his brother became King James II. Many powerful people in England were opposed to James becoming king because he had made it known that he was a Catholic.

With James II as king, Penn felt he was in position to lobby his friend to get a number of Quakers out of prison. Because of the efforts of Penn and others, and in part because James II felt religious persecution because of his Catholicism, in 1686, James II released a large number of religious dissidents from prison. Many of them were Quakers, and some had been in prison for as long as 15 years.

The opposition to having a Catholic king continued to grow in England, and in 1688, James II was forced to step down as king. This event is known as the Glori-

James II, shown in this early 19th-century engraving, ruled England from his brother's death in 1685 until he was replaced by William of Orange in 1688. *(Library of Congress, Prints and Photographs Division [LC-USZ62-92123])*

William and Mary ruled England, Scotland, and Ireland from 1689 until Mary's death in 1694. Afterward, William II ruled alone until his death eight years later. *(Library of Congress, Prints and Photographs Division [LC-USZ62-87571])*

ous Revolution, in part because no shots were fired. James was replaced as king by William of Orange, a Dutch Protestant who was married to James II's daughter, Mary. William and Mary ruled England together and were suspicious of many who had been supporters of her father, James II, and her uncle Charles II. William Penn fell into this group. William and Mary did not allow Penn to rule his colony, although they did let him remain owner of the land.

Fearing the wrath of the monarchs, William Penn went into hiding in England. Eventually, William and Mary relented and returned Penn's full authority in the colony. On September 9,

## Excerpt from the Charter of Privileges Granted by
## William Penn to the Inhabitants of Pennsylvania
### October 28, 1701

*BECAUSE no People can be truly happy, though under the greatest Enjoyment of Civil Liberties, if abridged of the Freedom of their Consciences, as to their Religious Profession and Worship: And Almighty God being the only Lord of Conscience, Father of Lights and Spirits; and the Author as well as Object of all divine Knowledge, Faith and Worship, who only doth enlighten the Minds, and persuade and convince the Understandings of People, I do hereby grant and declare, That no Person or Persons, inhabiting in this Province or Territories, who shall confess and acknowledge One almighty God, the Creator, Upholder and Ruler of the World; and profess him or themselves obliged to live quietly under the Civil Government, shall be in any Case molested or prejudiced, in his or their Person or Estate, because of his or their conscientious Persuasion or Practice, nor be compelled to frequent or maintain any religious Worship, Place or Ministry, contrary to his or their Mind, or to do or super any other Act or Thing, contrary to their religious Persuasion.*

1699, William Penn once again set sail for Pennsylvania. He had received many letters from his supporters and agents in the colony letting him know that there were a number of problems that had arisen during his long absence.

The greatest problem involved the colonial government. During the reigns of James II and William and Mary, many changes took place in the colonies. Many colonies lost their original charters and became royal colonies. James II had even gone as far as trying to combine all the New England colonies, New York, and New Jersey into one colony known as the Dominion of New England. Although the government of Pennsylvania was allowed more rights and privileges than any of the other colonies and was left alone by London, the people, especially those in the assembly, wanted more.

When Penn arrived back in Philadelphia in 1699, he listened carefully to all sides and opinions and then told the assembly that they could make any changes they wanted to the Frame of Government. However, the assembly had difficulty reaching an agreement on what changes they actually wanted to make. Penn stepped in, and on October 28, 1701, he presented the assembly with the new Charter of Privileges.

In addition to ensuring religious freedom, the Charter of Privileges gave the people of Pennsylvania more rights and freedom than any other people in the colonies had. The expanded democratic rights that Penn gave to the people of his colony became a model on which the founders of the United States created both the Declaration of Independence and the U.S. Constitution. However, Penn would not be able to see the effects of the Charter of Privileges on his colony.

England was once again in turmoil as James II's other daughter, Anne, ascended to the throne in 1702. Penn feared that Pennsylvania might be in jeopardy of losing its independence to the Crown. He went back to London to protect his colony.

Shown in a 1936 photograph, this building, constructed in the 1770s, served as a Quaker meetinghouse in Catawissa, Pennsylvania. *(Library of Congress, Prints and Photographs Division [HABS, PA, 19-CAT, 1-1])*

Unfortunately, William Penn never returned to Pennsylvania. Queen Anne remembered Penn as a friend to her father and was sympathetic to his cause. However, Penn's creditors were not as sympathetic. Establishing Pennsylvania had cost huge sums of money that had not been offset by the money raised in land sales. In addition, some of the people overseeing Penn's personal fortune had stolen much of it.

Penn found himself deeply in debt and unable to pay his creditors. He was put in debtor's prison for a year until his friends in the Quaker community were able to raise enough money to pay his debts. The year in prison had a terrible effect on Penn's health, and in 1712, he suffered a paralyzing stroke. He never fully recovered from the stroke and died six years later. His second wife, Hannah Penn, became Pennsylvania's governor on his death and was in charge of the colony until her own death in 1727. (She has been Pennsylvania's only woman governor.) Penn's son John held the position of governor after Hannah. He was followed by his brother Thomas, who remained governor until his death in 1775. In his desire to create a colony where a person could worship and live in freedom, William Penn created the place that would become the birthplace of an entire country devoted to his ideals.

# The Other Pennsylvanians

The first people to rush to Pennsylvania were Quakers from England, Wales, and Ireland. A number of Quakers and others who were already living elsewhere in the colonies moved to Pennsylvania. In addition, large numbers of people from other parts of Europe and with other religious beliefs also flooded into the colony, especially in the 18th century. Penn promoted his colony extensively throughout Britain and Europe, and the promise of cheap land and great liberties drew many.

## THE GERMANS

William Penn traveled throughout Europe in hopes of enticing people to follow him to Pennsylvania. One area where his message was especially well received was in what was called the Palatinate. This is now a part of Germany, but at the time Germany was made up of a number of independent feudal states, where people were bound to the land by the landowners. It was an area that had suffered from many years of war in the early part of the 17th century and would suffer again in the first decades of the 18th century. It was also an area where many of the more conservative Protestant sects had followings.

Many of the people who were attracted to Penn's description of a bountiful land where they could practice their religions openly were poor farmers and artisans. However, at least one

# Benjamin Franklin
## (1706–1790)

In October 1723, Benjamin Franklin became one of the many new arrivals in Pennsylvania. Born and raised in Boston, he left when he found it hard to get along as an apprentice in his older brother's print shop. Philadelphia provided the perfect opportunity for the inventive and hardworking young man. Within a few years, Franklin owned his own print shop and became one of the colony's leaders.

In 1729, he took over publishing the *Pennsylvania Gazette,* which allowed him to display his interesting and witty writings

Benjamin Franklin's printing press is housed in the Smithsonian Institution in Washington, D.C. *(Library of Congress, Prints and Photographs Division [LC-USZ62-90299])*

J O I N, or D I E.

Published in the *Pennsylvania Gazette* on May 9, 1754, Benjamin Franklin's warning, "Join or Die," urges American colonists to unite against the French and the Native Americans. The segments of the snake in the image each represent a colony. *(Library of Congress, Prints and Photographs Division [LC-USZ62-9701])*

upper-class, educated German was interested in what Penn had to say. Francis Daniel Pastorius (1651–1720) became the head of the Frankford Land Company and led 13 families to Pennsylvania. Pastorius bought a large tract of land just northwest of Philadelphia

*Note,* This ALMANACK us'd to contain but 24 Pages, and now has 36; yet the Price is very little advanc'd.

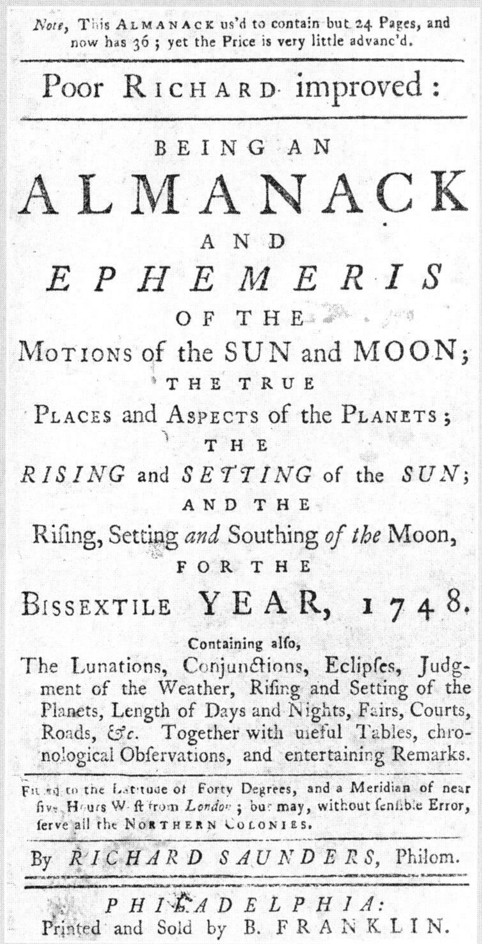

Poor RICHARD improved:

BEING AN

ALMANACK

AND

*EPHEMERIS*

OF THE

MOTIONS of the SUN and MOON;

THE TRUE

PLACES and ASPECTS of the PLANETS;

THE

*RISING* and *SETTING* of the *SUN*;

AND THE

Riſing, Setting *and* Southing *of the* Moon,

FOR THE

BISSEXTILE YEAR, 1748.

Containing alſo,

The Lunations, Conjunctions, Eclipſes, Judgment of the Weather, Riſing and Setting of the Planets, Length of Days and Nights, Fairs, Courts, Roads, &c. Together with uſeful Tables, chronological Obſervations, and entertaining Remarks.

Fitted to the Latitude of Forty Degrees, and a Meridian of near five Hours West from *London*; but may, without ſenſible Error, ſerve all the NORTHERN COLONIES.

By *RICHARD SAUNDERS*, Philom.

*PHILADELPHIA:*
Printed and Sold by B. FRANKLIN.

Benjamin Franklin began publishing *Poor Richard's Almanac* in 1732. The title page of the 1748 volume is shown here. *(Library of Congress, Prints and Photographs Division [LC-USZ62-75475])*

about life in the colonies. A few years later, in 1732, he began publishing *Poor Richard's Almanac.* Through these publications and his many other writings, Franklin became well respected throughout Pennsylvania and the rest of the colonies. Like many in Philadelphia at the time, Franklin was also interested in both natural and physical science. He amazed people with his electricity experiments. One of his experiments involved attaching a metal key to a kite string and using it to attract a lightning bolt. Based on his kite experiments, he invented lightning rods to protect buildings. He also invented a number of other useful items, including bifocal glasses and a type of woodstove made from iron that is still referred to as a Franklin stove.

As time went on, he became one of the leaders of the protests against British authority in the colonies. He was chosen as one of the five members of the Second Continental Congress to come up with the Declaration of Independence and was instrumental in the framing of the U.S. Constitution. During the American Revolution, Franklin represented the colonies in both Paris and London. Like many others of the time, his life had started somewhere else, but it was the spirit and opportunities available in Pennsylvania that allowed him to make a contribution to the creation of the United States.

and established the first German community in Pennsylvania in 1683. It was called Germantown.

Pastorius and his followers were Quakers. However, Germans from a number of other religious groups also came to Pennsylvania

After emigrating from Germany, Francis Daniel Pastorius, shown in a bas-relief (a sculpture that projects from a flat surface) located in Philadelphia, established the first German community in the city. *(Library of Congress, Prints and Photographs Division [LC-USZ62-96919])*

This poster promoting Lancaster County, Pennsylvania, advertises the costumes and handicrafts of the German Americans who settled there and whose descendants continue to live in much the same way. *(Library of Congress, Prints and Photographs Division [LC-USZC2-1869])*

in the 18th century. Amish, Mennonite, Moravian, Lutheran, Reformed, and other German Protestants flooded into Pennsylvania. By the time of the American Revolution, at least a third and possibly

## Excerpt from Pastorius's *Description of Pennsylvania*
### 1700

*As relating to our newly laid out town, Germanopolis, or Germantown, it is situated on a deep and very fertile soil, and is blessed with an abundance of fine springs and fountains of fresh water. The main street is sixty and the cross street forty feet in width. Every family has a plot of ground for yard and garden three acres in size.*

# Pennsylvania "Dutch"

It became common to refer to the German people of Pennsylvania as "Dutch." They were not Dutch in the sense of being from the Netherlands. The Germans refer to themselves in their own language as *Deutsch*. It is believed that their non-German-speaking neighbors mispronounced the word so that it sounded like "Dutch." Over time, this became the accepted way to refer to people of German descent in Pennsylvania. Even today, people refer to the Lancaster County area as "Pennsylvania Dutch country."

Swiss and German settlers in Pennsylvania often painted decorations on their barns called hex signs. They used different colors and shapes to represent everything from good fortune and fertility to hospitality and courage. This 1942 photograph of a barn wall in the vicinity of Terre Hill, Pennsylvania, shows hex signs on either side of an image of a cow. *(Library of Congress, Prints and Photographs Division [LC-USF34-082341])*

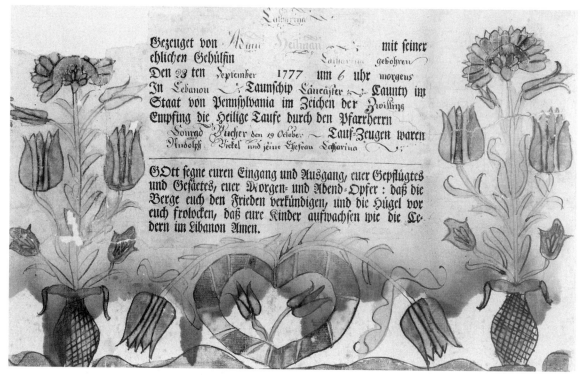

This birth and baptismal certificate for Catharina Heilman, born in 1777, in Lebanon, Pennsylvania, demonstrates the German presence in the colony. *(Library of Congress, Prints and Photographs Division [LC-USZ62-93917])*

In this 1941 photograph, Amish residents of Lancaster County, Pennsylvania, ride in an open buggy. *(National Archives, Still Picture Records [NWDNS-83-G-37607])*

as many as half of the people in the colony were of German descent. The Amish and Mennonites have very similar beliefs to the Quakers, and they settled in southeastern Pennsylvania. Many of their descendants are still in Lancaster County and the surrounding area. Today, some of these people live in much the same way as the original 18th-century German settlers. They have chosen to live without modern conveniences such as electricity. They still travel in horse-drawn carriages and dress in the plain fashion of their colonial forbears.

Due to the large concentration of German-speaking settlers in Pennsylvania, people continued to speak German for many generations. Printers in Germantown put out a German-language newspaper using paper made in the paper mill owned in part by a German, William Rittenhouse. In fact, in 1743, the first Bible printed in North America was printed by Christopher Saur in Germantown using Rittenhouse paper. The Bible was printed in German. There would not be an English-language Bible printed in North America until after the American Revolution. Many other aspects of German culture were brought to Pennsylvania and have become a part of the fabric of the United States.

The people of Germantown and the other German communities were at the forefront of social issues in the colony. As early as 1688, the people of Germantown let it be known that they believed slavery was against the ideals of Christianity. Their anti-slavery resolution was adopted by the town government. It was the

William Rittenhouse, the first paper maker in colonial America, built this house in 1707 in Philadelphia after emigrating from Germany. It was passed down in his family the following century. Rittenhouse's paper mill was located on a stream near his house. *(Library of Congress, Prints and Photographs Division [HABS, PA, 51-GERM, 78-9])*

first official statement against slavery in the colonies. Their protests went unheeded by Penn, who owned slaves, and most of the English-speaking people in the colony. The influence of the Germantown Resolution was felt by Germans throughout the colony, and almost no Germans owned slaves.

## SLAVES AND INDENTURED SERVANTS

Despite Penn's ideas about equality, he condoned and took advantage of two institutions of the time that are hard for people today to understand. Owning slaves and using indentured servants were both common practices in Pennsylvania. The first slaves in the British colonies arrived in Virginia in 1619, and the practice of owning slaves became common wherever large farms and plantations existed, especially in the southern colonies.

Although Native Americans were forced into slavery in some colonies, the majority of the slaves in the English colonies were people from Africa. The slave trade and slavery are a difficult part of the history of the United States for people today to understand. However, for a person such as William Penn, who believed in equality and freedom for all, slavery was acceptable for a number of reasons. Among the mistaken beliefs of slavery's supporters was the idea that to deserve the "inalienable rights" that come from God one had to believe in God. And one had to believe in the Christian god. Jews were tolerated in Pennsylvania but were denied the full rights given to Christian members of the colony.

Because the Africans brought as slaves to the colony were not Christians, many people believed it was all right to keep them as slaves, have separate laws for them, and treat them as property. Many of the slaves in Pennsylvania worked as servants for the wealthier people in the colony. Many other slaves worked as farm laborers. The slave population of Pennsylvania never exceeded 6 percent of the total population. In some of the southern colonies, there were more slaves than whites. In Virginia, which was the largest colony, the percentage of slaves was as high as 44 percent of the total population.

Just above slaves in social status in the colony were indentured servants. An indentured servant was someone who agreed to work for a period of time, usually around five years, in exchange for passage to America. For many poor people in Europe, this was the

# The Slave Trade

The first Africans brought to Virginia, in 1619, arrived on a Dutch ship. The Dutch were very active in the slave trade. However, as slavery became a major source of labor in the English colonies, the English and a number of colonials participated in the trade. Before the United States outlawed the importation of slaves, 10 million Africans had been forced to leave their homes and sold into slavery in America.

Hundreds of slaves were crowded into dark, tight quarters on the slave ships. On the way from Africa to the Americas, many died. The dead were unceremoniously thrown overboard when the ship's crew discovered them. Families that had not been broken up in Africa were often sold separately at auction in the Americas. Many slave owners in North America preferred to buy slaves who had already been worked on the plantations of the Caribbean. They believed that these slaves were less likely to cause problems.

The Dutch were only one of the European empires involved in the transatlantic slave trade during the 17th century. In 1637, as shown in this illustration from a 1671 Dutch book, they captured Elmina, a fort on the coast of West Africa, from which they transported slaves to their sugar plantations in Brazil. *(Library of Congress, Rare Book and Special Collections Division)*

only way they could get to the colonies. People who wanted to immigrate to Pennsylvania or one of the other colonies would sign an agreement bonding them to the person who paid for their passage. Often, someone on the ship held the indenture papers and would sell them when the ship arrived in the colonies, in effect "selling" the indentured servant.

Indentured servants did not have the same rights as other people and were often mistreated. Many of those who came to the colony as indentured servants did not survive long enough to become free. Others had their indentures extended if they tried to run away or their work was deemed unsatisfactory.

Many who headed to Pennsylvania to work as indentured servants died of disease or malnutrition during the voyage from Europe to America. On one ship loaded with 150 Germans, only 50 were still alive when the ship reached America. If a husband and wife were both indentured and one of them died during their passage, the survivor would have to serve the period of time of both indentures. If an entire family agreed to indenture and the parents died at sea, the children would remain indentured until they were 21 and were expected to pay for the passages of their dead parents.

For many others, though, starting their new lives in America as indentured servants worked out fine. After completing their time of indenture, many of these people moved to the frontier. Land was cheapest there, and often people were able to prosper if they were willing to work hard. When land in Pennsylvania became harder to get, many former indentured servants from Pennsylvania ended up moving south and living in the backcountry of both North and South Carolina.

## THE SCOTS-IRISH

Another large group that came to Pennsylvania during this time was the Scots-Irish. In 1607, after England defeated the Irish in a war, the king of England, James I, transplanted a large population of Scots from Scotland to the northern part of Ireland known as Ulster. The thinking at the time was that the Scots would take over the area inhabited by the most troublesome of the Irish and turn it into a prosperous area. Although it was not a good situation for the Irish people of the area (the two sides continue to oppose each other in Northern Ireland today), James I achieved his goal.

By the 18th century, many of the Scots in Ireland had grown dissatisfied with their situation. Landlords raising their rents, bad weather, livestock diseases, and crop failures forced many Scots-Irish to consider moving. Most of the early Scots-Irish to arrive in the American colonies ended up in Pennsylvania and Maryland. Many came as indentured servants.

It has been estimated that as many as 200,000 Scots-Irish left Ulster for America during the 18th century. They brought with them the Scottish ideas of thrift and hard work embodied in their Presbyterian version of Protestantism. Their beliefs were similar to the Quakers in that they lived and dressed in a simple and austere fashion. However, the Scots-Irish were not pacifists. It has been said that they settled the frontier with a Bible in one hand and a rifle in the other, and they were quick to turn to whichever one the situation called for.

Because much of the eastern part of the colony was already settled when the Scots-Irish arrived, many of them settled in the west. It was the Scots-Irish who were the first to settle west of the Allegheny Mountains, and it was there

King of Scotland from infancy, James I inherited the English throne when Elizabeth I died in 1603. He ruled England and Ireland until his death in 1625. *(Library of Congress, Prints and Photographs Division [LC-USZ62-105812])*

that they ran into problems with Native Americans and the Quakers. The American frontier, even when it was still east of the Mississippi River, was always a place where the people arrived ahead of the government. The Scots-Irish often settled on land that they neither bought from William Penn's agents nor from the Native Americans they displaced. It was the Scots-Irish on the frontier of Pennsylvania who first came into conflict with the French prior to the French and Indian War (1755–62).

After the French and Indian War, the Scots-Irish became some of the strongest and most vocal supporters of the protests against British authority. Some went so far as to refer to the American Revolution as the "Scots-Irish Uprising." The support by the Scots-

## The Walking Purchase

When William Penn negotiated the purchase of land from the Lenni Lenape, it was agreed that he would get the land along the Delaware River extending north as far as a man could walk in three days. At the time, a group led by Penn walked about 40 miles in a day and a half. In 1737, Thomas Penn decided to claim the rest of the land his father had purchased. This time, however, instead of a normal walking pace, the younger Penn turned it into a race with a prize for the person who could travel the farthest in 36 hours. The winner of the prize, Edward Marshall, covered 66 miles, and the Lenni Lenape felt cheated.

As time went on, more and more Native American land was taken by trickery or force. By the middle of the 18th century, the Native Americans of the colony, to whom Penn had guaranteed rights, were seen as an obstacle to the growth of the colony.

Irish for the American Revolution is easily understood. Their ancestors had been forced to leave Scotland for Ireland. Their mistreatment by the Crown in Ireland had forced many of them to Pennsylvania and the other American colonies. It was here that they would be pushed no further by a monarch who cared little for their well-being.

## OTHER SETTLERS

The Quakers, the various German groups, and the Scots-Irish made up the vast majority of the people in Pennsylvania. However, other groups also came to the colony to share in its freedom and religious toleration. French Protestants known as Huguenots were persecuted by the Catholic majority in France and had left that country in large numbers. Some had moved to the Protestant countries in Europe and then followed immigrants from those areas to the American colonies. Some Huguenots found their way to Pennsylvania after first living in the Palatinate area of Germany.

Maryland had been set up as a haven for Catholics seeking to start a new life in America. However, the liberal laws and low-priced land in Pennsylvania attracted a number of French and Irish Catholics to Pennsylvania. Even though William Penn had

The Society of Friends, also known as Quakers, traces its roots to George Fox's preaching about an "inner light" that all people have, which he claimed was the manifestation of Christ in each person. This early 19th-century watercolor shows a traveler's interpretation of a Quaker. *(National Archives of Canada)*

restricted participation in government to those who practiced a Christian religion, the colony was relatively tolerant of all beliefs. Because of this, a number of Jews settled in Philadelphia. The Jews who settled in Pennsylvania soon became respected members of the colony.

All these people created pressure for the colony to expand ever westward. Land-hungry Pennsylvanians soon began to ignore Penn's original statements about treating the Native Americans fairly. Conflicts arose and land was taken without treaties or payment. In addition, a number of land companies in Virginia claimed lands in what is now western Pennsylvania. Both the Virginians and Pennsylvanians bumped into a new problem in the West. The French, from what is now Canada but was at the time called New France, had come up the Great Lakes and then moved into the Ohio River Valley. Once there, they built forts in what would eventually be western Pennsylvania. The area claimed by these conflicting groups became the main battleground for the French and Indian War.

# 5

# The French and Indian War

## 1755–1762

Between 1689 and 1762, France and England went to war four times. The first three of these wars were fought primarily in Europe but spilled over into the two countries' colonies around the world. In North America, these four wars are referred to as the French and Indian Wars. The first three were also referred to in the English colonies in North America by the name of the person who sat on the British throne at the time of the war. The first was King William's War (1689–97). This was followed by Queen Anne's War (1702–13). The third war was known as King George's War (1744–48). The fourth and final war in this series of conflicts was called the Seven Years' War in Europe, while in North America it was called the French and Indian War (1755–62).

In North America, the first three wars were primarily border skirmishes between the French who had settled along the Saint Lawrence River Valley and the English colonies of New York and New England. The French never settled in large numbers and depended on the fur trade to create wealth in New France. After King George's War, the French had expanded their claims from the Saint Lawrence to include a vast territory surrounding the Great Lakes and south down the Mississippi River to the French settlement of New Orleans on the Gulf of Mexico. The claims by the

French effectively cut off the western expansion of the English colonies. Some of these colonies had been granted charters that gave them land that went from the Atlantic to the Pacific Ocean.

The peace-loving Quakers in Philadelphia cared little about the French expansion to their west. When a French expedition traveled throughout the upper reaches of the Ohio River in 1749, expedition members planted numerous lead plaques in the ground at many locations in order to establish the French claim to the area, but there was little or no reaction in Philadelphia. In 1752, the marquis de Duquesne arrived in New France as the governor and immediately set about strengthening the French claim in the Ohio River Valley. As soon as the ice was out of the Saint Lawrence in spring 1753, a force of 2,000 French soldiers and their Indian allies headed up the Saint Lawrence by boat. After traveling up Lake Ontario, they crossed Lake Erie to a spot where they began construction of Fort Presque Isle, near modern-day Erie, Pennsylvania.

From there, they moved inland a short distance, near what is now Waterford, Pennsylvania. Here they built Fort Le Boeuf—the first in a series of forts in the headwaters of the Ohio River—out of the logs they cut as they cleared the area. Once Fort Le Boeuf was established, they sent some of their force back to Erie to complete Fort Presque Isle to protect their landing spot on Lake Erie. They then built more forts along the waterways that led to the Ohio River. In spring 1754, at the point where the Allegheny and Monongahela Rivers join to form the Ohio River, the French built Fort Duquesne, their largest fort in western Pennsylvania.

At this time, William Penn's family was living in England and may not have had much interest in the western reaches of the colony. The Quakers, who controlled the politics of Pennsylvania, refused to take any warlike actions against the French. At the same time, Virginia also claimed some of the lands in the Ohio River Valley. The Ohio Company had been set up by a group of Virginians to sell land in the west. It fell to the Virginians to challenge the French in the Ohio River Valley.

## VIRGINIA STARTS A WAR IN PENNSYLVANIA

Robert Dinwiddie, who was the governor of Virginia at the time, decided to do what was necessary to protect Virginia's interests in the region of the Ohio. His first response was to send a young surveyor named George Washington, who was familiar with the western reaches of Virginia, to take a message to the French. Washington was 21 years old when he left Williamsburg, Virginia, on October 31, 1753, to take a message to the French at Fort Le Boeuf. Washington was a major in the Virginia Militia as well as a planter and surveyor. He traveled west with a group that included Christopher Gist as his scout and two French interpreters.

Washington reached Fort Le Boeuf on December 11, 1753. After a cordial dinner with the fort's commander, Jacques Legardeur de Saint-Pierre, Washington delivered his message that the French were to leave the vicinity of the Ohio and return to New France. Saint-Pierre politely refused and Washington headed back to Virginia. He reported to the governor on January 16, 1754. The governor was ready to take immediate action. Washington told him that he had passed the perfect site for a fort during his trip. It

Fort Necessity, near present-day Uniontown in southwestern Pennsylvania, was the location of the first battle of the French and Indian War. The reconstructed fort, shown in this contemporary photograph with a visitors' center visible in the background, consists primarily of a storehouse surrounded by a stockade, ditches, and mounds of dirt. *(National Park Service)*

## The Albany Congress
### 1754

In June and July 1754, representatives from New York, New Hampshire, Massachusetts, Rhode Island, Connecticut, Maryland, and Pennsylvania met with the leaders of the Iroquois Confederation in Albany, New York. The congress had two primary objectives. First, they wanted to appease the Iroquois and make sure they did not join the French. The delegates also wanted to come up with a united plan for defending the colonies against the French.

Benjamin Franklin was one of the delegates from Pennsylvania. Franklin wanted the congress to go even further. He pro-posed that the colonies band together into a union that would be able to deal with issues that affected all the colonies, especially their common defense. Franklin's ideas, known as the Albany Plan, were presented to most of the colonial legislatures. None of the colonies agreed to the Albany Plan. However, it was the first time that the colonists considered forming a union. Some historians believe that Franklin got some of his ideas for the Albany Plan from the Iroquois's own arrangement in their League of Five Nations.

was on a point of land where the Allegheny and the Monongahela Rivers join to form the Ohio River.

Governor Dinwiddie took immediate action. Workers and a small militia force were sent out to build the fort. They reached the spot Washington had seen during the winter and began to clear the site. On April 16, 1754, a large French force arrived and the Virginians building the fort were forced to surrender. The French completed the work and called their new post Fort Duquesne. Meanwhile, Washington had been promoted to lieutenant colonel by the governor and was given command of a force of about 150 soldiers. They were to join the other Virginians at the fort.

Fortunately for the colonials, not all the Indians in the area were allied with the French, and Washington was warned that the French, not the Virginians, were awaiting his arrival. About 20 miles from Fort Duquesne, near present-day Uniontown, on May 28, 1754, Washington's force surprised a party from Fort Duquesne. In the battle that followed, the Virginians killed 10 of the French soldiers, including the officer in charge. This first battle of the French and Indian War is known as the Battle of Great Meadows. It was the only victory for the English side for quite a while.

After the battle, Washington had his men hastily throw up defenses, which they named Fort Necessity. After a few more skirmishes between the Virginians and the French, a French force of more than 1,000 surrounded Fort Necessity on July 3, 1754. Washington had fewer than 400 men when the battle started and from the fort they were able to kill or wound many of the French. However, the Virginians suffered many casualties as well. More than 100 of Washington's men were either dead or wounded. The Americans inside the fort were also low on supplies. Washington realized there was nothing to be gained by trying to hold the fort, so he surrendered. Fortunately for Washington and his men, the French allowed them to return to Virginia. The French were clearly in control of the Ohio.

## REDCOATS VERSUS FRONTIER FIGHTERS

In Europe in the middle of the 18th century, warfare was a formal undertaking. The forces from both sides would line up in an orderly fashion and begin firing at each other. The battle would continue until one side or the other gave way. It was considered cowardly to fire from behind cover or to ambush one's enemies. In North America, during the many battles between colonists and Native Americans and in the three previous French and Indian Wars, a different style of warfare had developed. It involved surprise attacks, sharpshooters firing from cover, and other tactics learned from the Native Americans.

In January 1755, Major General Edward Braddock arrived in Virginia with 1,000 regular army troops, most of whom were Irish. His orders were to remove the French from the Ohio River area. Braddock enlisted George Washington as his aide and began to move his force along with all their supplies and artillery toward Fort Duquesne. Braddock had never been in the colonies and had no idea how difficult it would be to move his army into the west.

The British expected the colonials to assist the general, and Virginia provided men and supplies. Braddock had nothing but contempt for the ill-clad and loosely disciplined colonial militia. He turned down the offer of help from Native Americans who were loyal to the British side. The government of Pennsylvania still refused to take any warlike action. However, after much heated debate, Benjamin Franklin convinced the assembly to provide food and other supplies to Braddock. Franklin bought 150 Conestoga wagons and 600 horses to move the supplies to Cumberland, Maryland, where Braddock prepared his force for their march into the wilderness.

When Braddock arrived in Virginia, he had no idea where Fort Duquesne was, nor did he realize that there was no road to take him there. On June 7, 1755, Braddock's force left Cumberland, Maryland. It was almost 100 miles from Cumberland to Fort Duquesne, and woodsmen had to clear the way ahead of the army, allowing it to travel less than three miles a day. Indian scouts from Fort Duquesne must have found it easy to keep track of Braddock's progress. They also made a habit of using their tomahawks on anyone who wandered into the woods away from the main force.

Captain Daniel de Beaujeu commanded Forts Niagara, Detroit, and Duquesne. *(National Archives of Canada)*

By the time Braddock got close to Fort Duquesne on July 9, 1755, the French had long been aware he was coming and knew exactly what his force was like. The French commander, Captain Daniel de Beaujeu, was extremely concerned. He had a force of approximately 700 French and Indian fighters to defend the fort, while Braddock had 1,400 men, including the militia. In addition, Braddock had enough artillery with him to turn the wooden fort into matchsticks if the cannons were put into place. Beaujeu saw only one chance and that was to attack the English before they were set up.

On June 9, Captain Beaujeu came out to confront the British troops, who were spread out over a couple of miles on their new road. When the French charged, the British were thrown into confusion. Captain Beaujeu died in the first charge, but his subordinates rallied the French forces, who took to the woods on either side of Braddock's road. General Braddock refused to allow his men to take cover, forcing them to remain in their tight formations

# Conestoga Wagons

In the Conestoga region of Pennsylvania, settlers in the early 18th century devised a new style of wagon for moving large amounts of freight from their farms to market. This four-wheeled wagon was pulled by either four or six horses and had a hoop frame covered with canvas to protect the freight. A Conestoga wagon could carry about seven tons of cargo. Before the railroads were built in the late 19th century, the Conestoga wagon was the primary way of moving goods overland. When families moved west, they would load all their belongings into one of these wagons and head out for the frontier. In the 19th century, as the United States pushed westward beyond the Mississippi River, a version of these wagons called prairie schooners was used extensively.

Conestoga wagons were developed by some Pennsylvania colonists during the early 18th century. This particular wagon was photographed in 1900. *(Library of Congress, Prints and Photographs Division [LC-USZ62-113101])*

as the French and Indians mowed them down. The battle was so intense that Braddock had four horses shot out from under him. While on his fifth horse, a bullet dealt the general a fatal blow.

This is known as the Battle of the Wilderness, and the English learned a costly lesson. More than 1,000 English and colonial soldiers were killed or wounded. The French casualties numbered fewer than 100. In the woods of North America, standing one's ground out in the open was the way to sure defeat, even with twice as many troops. Some have written that the remnants of Braddock's army did not stop running until they reached Philadelphia. Washington wrote, "We have been most scandalously beaten by a trifling body of men."

After the Battle of the Wilderness, it looked like the French were going to win the war. They had other victories in New York and New England, and the frontier of Pennsylvania became easy pickings for France's Native American allies. Settlements and homesteads were raided and burned. Settlers were killed and scalped or taken prisoner. Pennsylvania's governor, Robert Hunter Morris, and his council offered a bounty on Native American scalps. At the same time, under the leadership of Benjamin Franklin, the Pennsylvania assembly had dozens of forts built along the frontier.

## PITT WINS THE WAR

In part because of the failure to secure the colonies, a new government came into power in London. The new prime minister was William Pitt, and he was determined to drive the French out of North America, no matter the cost. In 1758, British general John Forbes arrived in Philadelphia with 8,000 soldiers and orders to capture Fort Duquesne. George Washington was once again recruited to make his fourth trip into the west. He no doubt hoped that it would turn out better than his first three.

Although Forbes lost 300 men in his advance unit when they went against orders and got within the range of the fort, the overwhelming size of his force was more than the French were willing to fight. The French blew up Fort Duquesne and headed back to the Saint

William Pitt began his service in Parliament in 1735 and gained more power, becoming the prime minister during the French and Indian War. *(Library of Congress, Prints and Photographs Division [LC-USZ62-55013])*

Lawrence. Forbes instructed his men to build a new fort on the site. He named it Fort Pitt after the prime minister who had decided to win the war. The town that quickly grew up around the fort was named Pittsburgh.

After abandoning the Ohio watershed, the French also suffered defeats in New York and New England. In 1759, the British took the fight into the heart of New France, first capturing Quebec and then Montreal. Under the Treaty of Paris, which was finally signed by both sides in 1763, all of North America east of the Mississippi River and much of what is now western Canada were united as part of the British Empire. Although the French had surrendered, many of their Native American allies were not ready to give up.

During the French and Indian War, the British forces built Fort Pitt on the site of Fort Duquesne (in the vicinity of present-day Pittsburgh) after the French destroyed Fort Duquesne. This building, currently used as a museum and gift shop, is the only surviving original structure from Fort Pitt. *(Library of Congress, Prints and Photographs Division [HABS, PA,2-PITBU,20-2])*

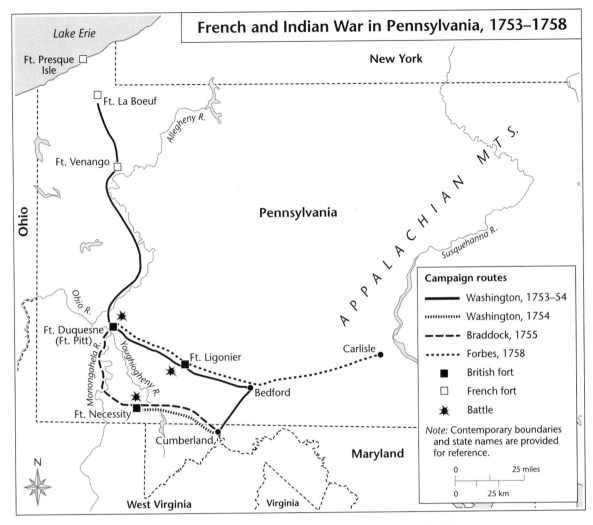

### French and Indian War in Pennsylvania, 1753–1758

Lake Erie

Ft. Presque Isle

New York

Ft. La Boeuf

Allegheny R.

Ft. Venango

Ohio

Pennsylvania

A P P A L A C H I A N   M T S.

Susquehanna R.

Ohio R.

Ft. Duquesne (Ft. Pitt)

Monongahela R.

Youghiogheny R.

Ft. Ligonier

Carlisle

Bedford

Ft. Necessity

Cumberland

Maryland

N

West Virginia

Virginia

**Campaign routes**

— Washington, 1753–54

‧‧‧‧‧‧‧ Washington, 1754

– – – Braddock, 1755

‧‧‧‧‧ Forbes, 1758

■ British fort

□ French fort

✳ Battle

*Note:* Contemporary boundaries and state names are provided for reference.

| 0 | 25 miles |
| 0 | 25 km |

The area that became western Pennsylvania was one of the major battlegrounds of the war.

## PONTIAC'S REBELLION

In 1762, Pontiac, the war chief of the Ottawa, organized the tribes in the area around Fort Detroit and began attacking the British on May 9, 1763. With the aid of Neolin, a Lenni Lenape spiritual leader, Pontiac was able to convince many Native Americans that it was time to rise up against the English and the colonists. The fighting soon spread throughout the Great Lakes area and along the frontiers of Virginia and Pennsylvania. Warriors from the Shawnee, Miami, Potawatomi, Seneca, and Lenni Lenape joined Pontiac and

Pontiac, leader of the Ottawa, organized attacks on English forts and settlements in the area surrounding Fort Detroit. In an attempt to reach a compromise, he met with Major Henry Gladwin, commander of the fort. Displeased with the results of their meetings, Pontiac led an attack on the fort but was ultimately defeated. *(National Archives of Canada)*

the Ottawa. Fort Detroit and Fort Pitt were both besieged. Once the British realized the seriousness of the rebellion, they sent forces to both Fort Pitt and Fort Detroit. When Pontiac and his followers learned that the French had signed a peace treaty with the British in 1763, many lost the will to fight. Those Native Americans who were in the area of Fort Detroit were weakened further by a small-pox epidemic that raged through their camps. In August 1763, Colonel Henry Bouquet and his 500 militiamen defeated a large

Native American force at the Battle of Bushy Run, near modern-day Greensburg, Pennsylvania, and the rebellion ended.

By fall 1764, the rebellion was over. During this time, many Native Americans were killed by war or disease, and many others moved even farther west. After Pontiac's Rebellion there were only about 1,000 Native Americans left in all of Pennsylvania. It looked like everything was going in the right direction for the colonies until the Crown decided it should help pay some of the debt that London had amassed to defeat the French.

# 6

## The Road to Revolution

William Pitt's successful efforts to defeat France around the world resulted in an important victory for Great Britain. Canada, India, and many former French islands in the Caribbean were added to the British Empire. The Crown, however, had been forced to go into debt to supply its far-flung army and navy. After the Seven Years' War, the government in London was also faced with the increased cost of protecting and governing the additions to its empire. It seemed logical to the British government that the people of the colonies, especially those in North America, should help pay for the war and for the troops and Crown officials stationed there.

In the decade following the French and Indian War, Parliament passed a number of different laws aimed at taxing the North American colonies. In the process, the two sides grew to distrust and dislike each other to the point of war. In 1763, there were very few people in the colonies who would have even considered independence. In 1776, the delegates from the thirteen colonies signed the Declaration of Independence, and many people in the colonies were ready to fight for their freedom.

Before the people in Pennsylvania arrived at the position of wanting the independence demanded by more radical colonists in places such as Massachusetts and Virginia, they had to deal with an internal conflict. Politics in Pennsylvania had split into two contentious groups. The descendants of William Penn were still the proprietors of the colony and, through appointments, controlled the council and most government offices. Most of the Penns' followers were successful Quakers. The other side consisted at first of those who thought the colony would be better off if the Crown was in charge instead of the Penns.

Over time, many of the colonies changed their charters, ending the rule of individuals and companies and bringing the colonies under royal control. One of the people in favor of Pennsylvania becoming a royal colony was Benjamin Franklin. In the 1760s, Franklin spent much of his time in London, trying to convince Crown officials that it was time to end Penn's proprietorship. While Franklin was trying to convince the Crown to help his cause, he and others in Pennsylvania were at first reluctant to speak out against laws like the Sugar Act of 1763.

## THE SUGAR ACT
### April 5, 1764

Parliament had two goals when it passed the Sugar Act. First, the act was intended to reform the duties on imported sugar and molasses so the colonists would be inclined to trade legally with British colonies in the Caribbean that produced sugar and molasses. The other part of the law was designed to make it harder for the colonists to continue their illegal trade outside the British Empire. In many colonies, smuggling had become the regular way of doing business. Even during the French and Indian War, many New England merchants continued to trade with the French.

In places like Boston, where any interruption in the illegal sugar and molasses trade hurt business, merchants organized to protest the Sugar Act. However, the honest and hardworking Quaker merchants of Philadelphia believed in following the rules. Prior to the Sugar Act, there had been little or no smuggling on the Delaware. In addition, the molasses trade was not very important to Pennsylvania. Many merchants in New England had become involved in a complicated trade arrangement whereby they brought molasses from the Caribbean to New England and turned it into rum. The rum was then traded in Europe for manufactured goods. The Sugar Act failed to produce much in the way of revenue

Many British colonies in the Caribbean produced sugar from sugarcane. In this mid-18th-century British engraving, a white overseer directs Native peoples (possibly in the West Indies) while they process sugarcane. *(Library of Congress, Prints and Photographs Division [LC-USZ62-7841])*

for the Crown, so the government in London decided further steps were needed.

## THE STAMP ACT
### March 22, 1765

After the French and Indian War, the Crown decided that an army should be maintained in the colonies to help protect them. The British prime minister, George Grenville, estimated that it would cost about £200,000 a year to support the troops in North America. He also figured that the colonies should pay for their own protection.

To raise the money, Parliament passed the Stamp Act on March 22, 1765. Stamp taxes were nothing new at the time. They were in common use in England, and some of the colonies in North America used them. What created a huge reaction in the colonies was the fact that this was the first time that Parliament had passed a law that would directly tax the people in North America. People were further upset by the fact that there were no representatives from the colonies in Parliament. The idea of "no taxation without representation" became one of the rallying points of resistance to the Crown.

The Stamp Act was supposed to go into effect on November 1, 1765. Before that happened, the colonists let it be known that they would not stand idly by and accept this tax. The law called for stamps to be purchased and attached to many different types

When affixed to goods, this stamp signified that a tax must be paid upon purchase. Many colonists felt that the British unfairly introduced these taxes when they implemented the Stamp Act in 1765, which affected goods and services ranging from business transactions to playing cards. *(Library of Congress, Prints and Photographs Division [LC-USZ61-539])*

of legal documents, newspapers, and other printed material, as well as some consumer items such as playing cards. Stamp agents were appointed in each of the colonies, and they were to distribute the stamps once they arrived from England and the law went into effect. The stamp agents and other Crown officials became the targets of protests throughout the colonies led by groups known as the Sons of Liberty.

With the Stamp Act, Benjamin Franklin began to see that the Crown would be no better at governing Pennsylvania than the Penns were. In testimony before Parliament, Franklin claimed that although Parliament had the right to regulate the colonies, a direct tax such as the Stamp Act was unfair. In some colonies, stamp agents were burned or hanged in effigy. Protesters broke into the houses of stamp agents, and many agents resigned their jobs before they even began. As the time for the Stamp Act to go into effect drew near, the protests became more frequent. Many leaders in the colonies thought it was time for them to work together against the Stamp Act.

## Sons of Liberty

When the Stamp Act was passed by Parliament in 1765, people in the colonies formed groups in their communities to protest the act. One of the opponents of the Stamp Act in the House of Commons, Isaac Barré, called the protesters the "sons of liberty." Soon the name spread to the colonies, where it was readily adopted. Various Sons of Liberty groups organized protests against the Stamp Act and later held "tea parties" in such places as Boston, New Jersey, and South Carolina when the Tea Act was passed. The Sons of Liberty were also responsible for forming the Committees of Correspondence that kept the Patriots throughout the colonies up to date on what was occurring. The letters they passed around these local committees are credited with bringing about the First Continental Congress.

Colonists denounce the Stamp Act in 1765. *(Library of Congress)*

## THE STAMP ACT CONGRESS
### October 1765

In fall 1765, the Massachusetts General Court sent a letter to the other colonial assemblies suggesting that they send delegates to a meeting in New York City in October to discuss what actions they could take. At this point, everyone was looking for a way to solve the problem with Parliament. Nine of the colonies, including Pennsylvania, sent delegates to New York. The governors of Georgia, North Carolina, and Virginia refused to call their assemblies together to select delegates. The New Hampshire legislature supported the idea of the meeting but did not send anyone to represent the colony.

The idea of taxation without representation was the major topic of the congress. The delegates

John Dickinson represented Pennsylvania at the Stamp Act Congress. *(Library of Congress, Prints and Photographs Division [LC-USZ62-26777])*

agreed that Parliament had the right to regulate the empire. They did not believe that Parliament had the right to impose a direct tax on people who had no voice in the process. The delegates decided that their best course of action was to appeal directly to the king in the hope that he would intervene with Parliament. John Dickinson, one of the delegates from Pennsylvania, was one of the primary authors of the resolutions the congress sent to the king.

The protests over the Stamp Act and a change in government in London produced the desired effect. Georgia was the only colony that ever issued any of the stamps, and on March 18, 1766, the Stamp Act was repealed. The turmoil in the colonies subsided. The protest movement started by the Stamp Act might have faded away then; however, Parliament could not leave the colonies alone.

## THE TOWNSHEND DUTIES
### June 29, 1767

The failure of the Stamp Act and the need to give the people in England a large tax cut had the British government and Parliament looking for new ways to raise revenues. Charles Townshend, one of the leaders of the British government, took Benjamin Franklin's comments about the Stamp Act seriously. He decided that if a direct tax on the colonists was not going to work, he would come up with a series of indirect taxes on trade.

On June 29, 1767, Parliament passed a law, known as the Townshend Duties, that put a tax called a duty on a variety of goods imported into the colonies. Duties were placed on glass, lead, paper, painter's colors, and tea. Reaction to the law in the colonies was mixed. Some accepted the fact that Parliament was within its rights to impose these indirect taxes, but more radical elements in the colonies were not willing to accept any form of taxation without representation.

The Massachusetts legislature took the lead in the protest movement. They sent out what is now called the Circular Letter, asserting that Parliament had no right to tax people without representation. John Dickinson was once again in the middle of the radicals in Pennsylvania and soon came to prominence throughout the colonies. In 1767, Dickinson began sending letters to the *Pennsylvania Chronicle* and other newspapers throughout the colonies. Titled *Letters from a Pennsylvania Farmer*, they were published as a book in the same year. Dickinson argued against the authority of Parliament to impose any taxes or duties on the colonies. Many people in the colonies agreed to refuse to buy or import the goods listed in the Townshend Duties.

## Excerpt from the First *Letter from a Pennsylvania Farmer*, Written by John Dickinson

*From infancy I was taught to love humanity and liberty. Inquiry and experience have since confirmed my reverence for the lessons then given me by convincing me more fully of their truth and excellence. Benevolence toward mankind excites wishes for their welfare, and such wishes endear the means of fulfilling them. These can be found in liberty only, and therefore her sacred cause ought to be espoused by every man, on every occasion, to the utmost of his power. As a charitable but poor person does not withhold his mite because he cannot relieve all the distresses of the miserable, so should not any honest man suppress his sentiments concerning freedom, however small their influence is likely to be. Perhaps he may "touch some wheel" that will have effect greater than he could reasonably expect.*

Although the people in Pennsylvania were slow to join the nonimportation movement, people in Boston and New York had numerous clashes with British authority and the troops that had been sent to support them. On January 18, 1770, there were numerous injuries when protesters and British soldiers clashed in New York in what is known as the Battle of Golden Hill. On March 5, 1770, the first deaths in the clashes between Britain and its

Paul Revere's engraving of the Boston Massacre depicts the event that many consider the beginning of the struggle for independence. It occurred on March 5, 1770. *(Library of Congress, Prints and Photographs Division [LC-USZ62-35522])*

colonies took place in Boston. A mob of protesters began throwing snow and ice at British troops, who reacted by firing into the crowd. Five colonists died and six others were wounded in what is known as the Boston Massacre.

After the Boston Massacre, the leaders in London realized that the Townshend Duties were not only causing serious problems but had also failed to generate much in the way of revenue. In April 1770, all of the Townshend Duties, except the one on tea, were repealed. With the repeal of the duties, the situation in the colonies quieted down. However, by this time very few of the colonists felt British. Most had been born in America, and close to half of the people in the colonies did not even have English ancestors. People from Ireland and Scotland disliked the English, while people from other countries in Europe felt no allegiance to the British Crown. Anti-British feelings smoldered in the colonies until they were fanned into a full blaze over tea.

## THE TEA ACT
## May 10, 1773

In 1773, the British East India Company was on the verge of bankruptcy. Because the company had many supporters in the government, Parliament decided to try to help. On May 10, 1773, a law known as the Tea Act was passed that changed the way tea was to be imported. Before the Tea Act, the East India Company had to ship all its tea to England, where it was taxed and sold to tea merchants. The tea merchants then exported it to the colonies, where it would be resold at a profit. When it reached the colonies, merchants were required to pay the remaining Townshend duty. Then they, too, marked up the tea so they could make a profit. This made tea very expensive, and many people in the colonies either drank smuggled Dutch tea or made various "teas" using a variety of native plants.

Under the Tea Act, the British East India Company was given permission to ship tea directly to the colonies, avoiding the tax and the middlemen in England. Had the Tea Act been allowed to go into effect, English tea would have actually been cheaper in the colonies. However, many colonists did not like the idea of London giving one company a monopoly over the tea trade.

On December 16, 1773, after ships bearing the first load of tea arrived in Boston Harbor, 60 members of the Sons of Liberty,

To protest the passage of the Tea Act, some male colonists, disguised as American Indians, boarded three ships in Boston Harbor on December 16, 1773, and dumped hundreds of cases of tea into the harbor. The event became known as the Boston Tea Party. *(Library of Congress)*

disguised as Indians, went aboard the ships and dumped £10,000 worth of tea into the harbor. There were similar protests in other colonies. In Pennsylvania, even before the Boston Tea Party, word went out that the ship *Polly* was bringing tea to Philadelphia. The Sons of Liberty in Philadelphia told harbor pilots along the Delaware River to refuse to guide the *Polly* into port. They also sent a message to the ship's captain that they were waiting to put a "halter [noose] around [his] neck" and that they planned to cover him with "ten gallons of liquid tar" and "the feathers of a dozen geese." The practice of covering a person with tar and then feathers as punishment was known as being tarred and feathered.

The captain of the *Polly* did the prudent thing and turned his ship back toward England without reaching Philadelphia. At first, it looked like the protests of the colonists would once again defeat the powers of the British Empire. However, the Crown had had enough. Britain felt it was time to punish its misbehaving children in the North American colonies, and Parliament went to work fashioning a series of laws that would push the colonies into armed rebellion.

7

# Declaring Independence

## THE INTOLERABLE ACTS
## 1774

After the Boston Tea Party, Parliament passed a series of laws that were intended to force the American colonies into line. The British referred to them as the Coercive Acts. However, in America they were seen in a different light and quickly came to be known as the Intolerable Acts. There were five parts to the Intolerable Acts, and the first is known as the Boston Port Bill, which was passed on March 31, 1774.

The Boston Port Bill closed the port of Boston to all shipping until someone paid for the tea that had been dumped in the harbor. Although many people knew exactly who had been involved, none had any intention of giving in to the Crown. With the harbor closed, the people in Boston were in a difficult situation. They could not last long without shipments of food and other necessary supplies.

The people of Philadelphia learned of the closing of Boston's port on May 18, 1774, when Paul Revere, a Boston silversmith and a member of the Sons of Liberty, rode into town spreading the word of Britain's increased hostilities. People throughout the colonies came to Boston's aid by sending supplies to nearby cities that were then shipped to Boston overland.

In Pennsylvania, word of the Crown's retaliation against the people of Boston caused many to take action. Under the leadership of radicals such as John Dickinson and others, the assembly chose a 19-member Committee of Correspondence to direct Pennsylvania's contact with Boston and the Patriot movement throughout the colonies. As the divide between the Crown and the colonies grew, the Committees of Correspondence functioned as the government for the Patriot side.

Many Quakers in Pennsylvania were reluctant to join the Patriot movement. The Society of Friends did not support the general work stoppage that was held on June 1, 1774, to protest the situation in Boston. But as the details of the other Intolerable Acts became known, more and more people were pushed toward some sort of action against the Crown.

The second Intolerable Act, known as the Massachusetts Government Act, which passed in Parliament on May 20, 1774, made it clear that the Crown felt the colonies were subject to the whims of the king and Parliament. This law changed the Massachusetts charter, taking away long-standing rights from the General Court, the courts, and even town governments. People in the colonies realized that their rights were in jeopardy.

The remaining three Intolerable Acts continued to strain the situation between the colonies and the Crown. The Administration of Justice Act, passed on May 20, 1774, allowed the Crown to pick the time and place of trials for anyone committing a crime against British laws. Under this law, royal authorities could even send an offender in the colonies to England to stand trial. The fourth law, the Quartering Act of June 2, 1774, added insult to injury by declaring that the people in the colonies would have to give up any empty housing they had to soldiers if the colony did not provide barracks.

The last law was passed on June 22, 1774, and was called the Quebec Act. It gave the French and other people living in Canada special privileges. But more important, it made the lands between the Appalachian Mountains and the Mississippi River part of Canada. Many of the colonies had already claimed land there and a number of settlers had already moved west of the mountains.

Many people were hard pressed to figure out what to do about the Intolerable Acts. Most still expected some sort of reconciliation with the Crown. There was one thing that most people agreed on, and that was the need for the colonies to work together to try and solve their differences with the king and Parliament. Word went

The Quebec Act, the last of the Intolerable Acts, extended Quebec into an area between the Ohio and Mississippi Rivers that many American colonists had already claimed. In this engraving, the prime minister of Great Britain and the lord chief justice celebrate the passage of the act. *(National Archives of Canada)*

out through the Committees of Correspondence that each colony should send a delegation to a congress to be held in Philadelphia, Pennsylvania, starting on September 5, 1774.

## THE FIRST CONTINENTAL CONGRESS
## September 5, 1774, to October 26, 1774

By 1774, Philadelphia was the largest and richest city in the colonies. It was close to the middle of the colonies geographically, so it was the logical location for what became known as the First Continental Congress. On September 5, 1774, 56 delegates representing 12 of the thirteen colonies were ready to work on a response to the king and Parliament. Only Georgia failed to send any delegates to the First Continental Congress.

The delegates represented a vast cross section of views and interests. Plantation owners from South Carolina had little in com-

## Loyalists, Patriots, and Undecideds

By the time fighting began in the colonies in spring 1775, the people were equally divided into three groups. The Patriots were ready and willing to fight for their rights and eventually for independence. The second group was made up of Loyalists, who were loyal to the king and wanted to remain British subjects. The final third were people who had yet to choose a side.

The First Continental Congress met in Philadelphia and composed and sent resolutions to the king of Britain. The delegates planned a second congress for the following spring to assess their situation. *(Library of Congress, Prints and Photographs Division [LC-USZ62-45328])*

mon with merchants from Boston, and the congress had the potential of breaking down over these differences. A Virginia Patriot, Patrick Henry, interrupted the debate at one point and told the group, "The distinctions between Virginians, Pennsylvanians, New Yorkers, and New Englanders are no more. I am not a Virginian but an American." Pennsylvania sent seven delegates to the congress, including John Dickinson, Thomas Mifflin, and Joseph Galloway. Galloway was elected the secretary of the meeting.

Galloway tried to lead the congress down a conciliatory path. He later broke with the Patriots and became a Loyalist once the Revolution began. He wanted the congress to come up with a proposal for a union of the colonies that would be under the direction of Parliament. For the more radical Patriots, this was unacceptable.

The congressional delegates made a declaration of what they thought were the rights of the people living in the colonies. They then drafted a series of resolutions to be sent to the king. These resolutions included an increasing number of economic sanctions against Britain, to be implemented if the complaints of the colonies were not addressed. Finally, they agreed to hold the Second Continental Congress in May 1775 to consider further action.

The king hardly considered the resolutions of the congress. The British military leaders in Boston were ordered to use force, if necessary, to bring the people of the area into line. Ben Franklin was

Patrick Henry was a powerful Revolutionary War leader who opposed complete independence from England. He represented the colony of Virginia at both the First and Second Continental Congresses. *(Library of Congress)*

## The Resolutions of the First Continental Congress

After listing numerous complaints with the attempts by Parliament to impose its will on the American colonies, the document sent to the king by the First Continental Congress made it clear that the Americans were planning boycott, not revolution.

*Resolved, unanimously, That from and after the first day of December next, there be no importation into British America, from Great Britain or Ireland of any goods, wares or merchandize whatsoever, or from any other place of any such goods, wares or merchandize.*

still in London when the First Continental Congress met in Philadelphia. When he became aware of the response to it in London, he knew the chances of settling the differences between the American colonies and Britain's king, George III, were remote. Franklin decided it was time to return to America. While he was making the voyage back to Philadelphia, and before the Second Continental Congress could convene, the situation between the British and the colonies turned violent.

## THE BATTLE OF LEXINGTON AND CONCORD
### April 19, 1775

Early on the morning of April 19, 1775, approximately 800 hand-picked British soldiers arrived on the town common in Lexington, Massachusetts. They had come to arrest some of the Patriot leaders who were reported to be in the area and to seize a supply of weapons that was supposedly hidden at a farm in nearby Concord. Instead, they found 70 minutemen waiting for them. Paul Revere and other riders from Boston had warned the minutemen that the British were on the move. When the British officer in charge ordered the colonials to surrender, they tried to run away. No one knows who fired first, but British soldiers got off two volleys before they stopped shooting. When the smoke from their muskets cleared the common, eight colonials were found dead and another 10 were wounded.

## Minutemen

Although the delegates at the First Continental Congress were still seeking a peaceful solution for their differences with the Crown, they did recommend that the colonies expand their militias, stockpile weapons, and start drilling their soldiers, just in case. Colonial militias had been in existence almost from the beginning and had been used in the early Indian wars and in the French and Indian Wars. The idea was to have a large number of people who could be ready to take up arms to defend themselves and their communities at a minute's notice. Because of this, these part-time soldiers were called minutemen.

The Battle of Lexington and Concord (shown here in a print based on a painting titled *The First Blow for Liberty,* by F. O. C. Darley) signaled the beginning of the Revolutionary War. *(National Archives, Still Pictures Branch [NWDNS-JKH-JH-3])*

When the British force reached the North Bridge in Concord, they were met by a much more substantial Patriot force and were forced to retreat all the way to Boston. Along the way, colonial sharpshooters killed or wounded 273 of the "redcoats," which is what the Patriots called the British soldiers because they wore bright red uniforms. When the delegates to the Second Continental Congress arrived in Philadelphia a few weeks later, the entire situation had changed.

## THE SECOND CONTINENTAL CONGRESS
## 1775–1789

The Second Continental Congress convened on May 10, 1775, and remained the governing body of the Patriots and then the united colonies until the U.S. Constitution was enacted in 1789. Fifty of the 65 delegates had also attended the First Continental Congress. Among the new delegates were Benjamin Franklin, representing

Pennsylvania, and John Hancock, representing Massachusetts. Hancock served as the first president of the Second Continental Congress, and a year later, in August 1776, he was the first person to sign the Declaration of Independence. However, before the congress could address the issue of independence, they had to deal with the more immediate problems of the siege of Boston.

After the Battles of Lexington and Concord, thousands of colonial militia had surrounded Boston and the British forces that held it. On June 17, 1775, the Battle of Bunker Hill made it clear that reconciliation was out of the question. At Bunker Hill in Charlestown, Massachusetts, colonial forces fought a major battle with the British army. Although the British ultimately drove the Patriot forces from Breed's Hill and Bunker Hill, 226 of their soldiers were killed and 828 wounded, while the colonials suffered 140 killed and 271 wounded. The British commanders had only a limited number of

The Second Continental Congress convened on May 10, 1775, and remained in session until the newly independent United States had a constitution. *(National Archives, Still Picture Records [NWDNS-148-CCD-35])*

soldiers available in North America and could not afford to "win" battles in which they sustained that many casualties.

In Philadelphia, one of the first official acts of the congress was to create the Continental army and appoint George Washington as commanding general. Washington and many of the soldiers who fought with him brought their experiences in the French and Indian War to bear on their struggle against the British. Washington's first task was to end the siege of Boston. He went north with soldiers from Maryland, Virginia, and Pennsylvania. By the following spring, using cannons that had been transported from Fort Ticonderoga, New York, on Lake Champlain, Washington was victorious. The British left Boston on March 17, 1776.

Even though most believed that further conflict was likely, many delegates were still not ready to vote for independence. One of the events that pushed many in the colonies toward declaring independence was the publishing of Thomas Paine's pamphlet *Common Sense*. In London, Paine (1737–1809) met Franklin, who encouraged him to immigrate to Philadelphia. In 1774, Paine became the editor of *Pennsylvania Magazine*. As the debate over independence raged, Patriot leaders suggested that Paine write about the reason why the colonies should become independent from Britain. Prior to the publication of *Common Sense*, the arguments had not been presented in terms that the average person could understand. Paine's pamphlet was an immediate success. It was published on January 10, 1776, and it sold 100,000 copies in the first three months. Some 500,000 copies would eventually be distributed. Considering that there were only 2.5 million people in the American colonies, that is an amazing number.

More than 500,000 copies of Thomas Paine's *Common Sense* were distributed, demonstrating the colonists' support for independence. *(National Archives/DOD, War & Conflict, #63)*

While *Common Sense* swayed public opinion in favor of independence and George Washington succeeded in Boston, his fellow Virginian Thomas Jefferson took the lead in Philadelphia. With help from Franklin and John Adams from Massachusetts, Jefferson wrote the document that would change the course of history. The

One of the first and boldest acts of the Second Continental Congress was to compose and sign the Declaration of Independence in summer 1776. *(Library of Congress)*

## Excerpt from *Common Sense*
### January 10, 1776

*As much hath been said of the advantages of reconciliation, which like an agreeable dream, hath passed away and left us as we were, it is but right, that we should examine the contrary side of the argument, and enquire into some of the many material injuries which these Colonies sustain, and always will sustain, by being connected with and dependant on Great Britain. To examine that connection and dependence on the principles of nature and common sense, to see what we have to trust to if separated, and what we are to expect if dependant.*

*I have heard it asserted by some, that as America hath flourished under her former connection with Great Britain, that the same connection is necessary towards her future happiness and will always have the same effect—Nothing can be more fallacious that this kind of argument:—we may as well assert that because a child hath thrived upon milk, that it is never to have meat, or that the first twenty years of our lives is to become a precedent for the next twenty. But even this is admitting more than is true, for I answer, roundly, that America would have flourished as much, and probably much more had no European power taken any notice of her. The commerce by which she hath enriched herself are the necessaries of life, and will always have a market while eating is the custom of Europe.*

*But she has protected us say some. That she hath engrossed us is true, and defended the Continent at our expence as well as her own is admitted; and she would have defended Turkey from the same motive viz. the sake of trade and dominion.*

## The First Paragraph of the Declaration of Independence

Thomas Jefferson of Virginia is given credit as being the primary author of the Declaration of Independence. He began it with the following paragraph:

*When in the Course of human events, it becomes necessary for one people to dissolve the political bands which have connected them with another, and to assume among the Powers of the earth, the separate and equal station to which the Laws of Nature and of Nature's God entitle them, a decent respect to the opinions of mankind requires that they should declare the causes which impel them to the separation.*

Declaration of Independence echoed many of the ideas on which William Penn had founded his colony.

In the process of approving the Declaration of Independence, the congress had agreed that each colony, no matter how many delegates it sent or how many people it represented, would have one vote. When the state delegations to the Second Continental Congress were polled on July 1, 1776, it looked like only nine states were ready to vote in favor of the Declaration of Independence. Only two delegates from Delaware were present, and one voted for and one against. The delegates from New York had been instructed not to vote until a vote was taken in the state assembly. The delegates from Pennsylvania and South Carolina voted against the Declaration. Most delegates believed that all the colonies had to agree.

The Pennsylvania delegation consisted of seven members. In the first vote, they voted four to three against independence. On July 2, when the delegations were again polled, John Dickin-

Robert Morris represented Pennsylvania at the Second Continental Congress. *(Library of Congress, Prints and Photographs Division [LC-USZ62-70976])*

son and Robert Morris did not vote, and the rest of the Pennsylvania delegation voted three to two in favor of independence. The South Carolina delegates said they would not stand alone and would vote with the 11 colonies that had already agreed to independence. The New York delegates still did not vote, but they assured the congress that they would vote in the affirmative as soon as they got the official go-ahead from home.

Thomas Jefferson is usually given credit for authorship of the Declaration of Independence, a facsimile of which is shown here. *(National Archives)*

# Pennsylvania's Signers of the Declaration of Independence
## August 2, 1776

Robert Morris George Clymer
Benjamin Rush James Smith
Benjamin Franklin George Taylor
John Morton James Wilson
George Ross

George Clymer signed the Declaration of Independence on behalf of Pennsylvania. *(Library of Congress, Prints and Photographs Division [LC-USZ62-111789])*

Shown in a painting by John Trumbull, James Wilson represented Pennsylvania at the Second Continental Congress and signed the Declaration of Independence on behalf of the colony. Wilson later served as one of the first Supreme Court justices. *(Library of Congress, Prints and Photographs Division [LC-USZ62-113377])*

On July 2, 1776, the delegates voted 12 to zero in favor of independence. Two days later, on July 4, 1776, the Declaration of Independence passed by the same vote and the idea of reconciling

The Liberty Bell, shown in an illustration published in *Harper's* in 1869, was rung when the Declaration of Independence was read to colonists in Philadelphia on July 8, 1776. *(Library of Congress, Prints and Photographs Division [LC-USZ62-78928])*

with Parliament and the Crown was set aside. On July 9, 1776, New York made the vote unanimous. Then, on August 2, 1776, a ceremony was held for the delegates to sign the Declaration of Independence. As president of the congress, John Hancock was the first of 56 delegates to sign.

Copies of the Declaration of Independence were circulated and read throughout the colonies. When the Declaration was read to the people of Philadelphia on July 8, 1776, a large bell was rung. That bell is now called the Liberty Bell and is on display in Independence National Historic Park in Philadelphia. Throughout the colonies, many people rallied to the cause of independence. Many others still wanted to remain loyal to the Crown. Some of the Loyalists headed for British strongholds such as New York City, while others left for Canada or England. It took more than a declaration to make the colonies independent. It took a long and costly war before they became the United States.

# 8

# The War for Independence

After driving the British out of Boston in spring 1776, George Washington moved the Continental army south to Long Island and New York City. The colonials suffered a number of defeats in and around New York, and Washington was forced to retreat all the way across New Jersey. He and his army would have been captured by the British had he not crossed the Delaware River into Pennsylvania, making sure that were no boats left on the New Jersey side that the British could use to follow him. However, Washington was not ready to stay in Pennsylvania. He crossed back into New Jersey and won the Battle of Trenton and Princeton just as 1776 ended and 1777 began.

Washington kept his army in New Jersey for the rest of the winter of 1777. Throughout the spring and early summer of 1777, the British and colonial forces clashed a number of times in minor skirmishes, but Washington felt his army was not ready to take on the British in pitched battles. In July, the British commander General Sir William Howe decided to change his tactics. Instead of trying to fight his way across New Jersey to capture Philadelphia, he decided to move his men by ship and approach Philadelphia from the south.

## THE BATTLE OF BRANDYWINE

After the middle of July 1777, General Howe left New York on 260 ships with 18,000 men under his command. None of the

Patriots knew for sure where or when the British would show up next, but Washington was pretty sure they were headed for Philadelphia. About a month later, news came to Washington that Admiral Richard Howe's fleet had entered Chesapeake Bay. The British landed at the head of the Elk River in Maryland and then began to move toward Philadelphia.

George Washington and his troops surprised the British and Hessians at Trenton by attacking them the morning after Christmas Day, 1776.
*(National Archives/DOD, War & Conflict, #69)*

# Betsy Ross
## (1752–1836)

In 1870, William Canby attended a meeting of the Historical Society of Pennsylvania and claimed that his grandmother, Betsy Ross, had made the first American flag. He stated that in June 1776, George Washington, Robert Morris, and Ross's brother-in-law Colonel George Ross visited her upholstery shop on Arch Street in Philadelphia. Washington brought a sketch for a new flag that included red and white stripes and a blue corner with 13 stars. Washington had in-cluded six-pointed stars in his sketch. Supposedly, Betsy Ross suggested that they change them to five-pointed stars and then proceeded to make the first American flag. Although Canby could not substantiate his claim, a later examination of the shop's records revealed that Ross had in fact made a number of flags for people and was acquainted with George Washington. Although the truth is not known, Ross is generally given credit for sewing the first American flag.

It is generally believed that Betsy Ross sewed the first American flag. In this early 20th-century painting, Ross and two young women display the U.S. flag for George Washington and three other men. *(Library of Congress, Prints and Photographs Division [LC-USZ62-1767])*

General Nathanael Greene was a powerful and able leader during the Revolutionary War. *(National Archives/DOD, War & Conflict, #57)*

General Anthony Wayne was one of the military leaders George Washington counted on during the Revolutionary War. *(Library of Congress, Prints and Photographs Division [LC-USZ62-5667])*

At first, Washington sent out small forces intended to harass the British. The first skirmish was fought near Iron Hill, Delaware, on September 3. Having no choice but to defend Philadelphia as the symbolic capital of the yet unnamed independent country, Washington moved his army into position, using Brandywine Creek as a barrier between his army and the British. General Nathanael Greene from Rhode Island and General Anthony Wayne from Pennsylvania were given the job of defending the center of the Patriot position. Unfortunately, Washington received poor intelligence about the movements of Howe's forces.

On September 11, the leader of Howe's hired Hessian soldiers, Wilhelm von Knyphausen, attacked Greene and Wayne's troops with artillery fire. This was intended to be a diversion while General Howe moved his main force to Jeffry's Ford, where they crossed the Brandywine and attacked Washington's right flank. Outflanked and outmanned, Washington used the dark of night to retreat to Chester, Pennsylvania.

After winning the Battle of Brandywine, Howe played a game of cat and mouse as he tried to corner Washington's army into another pitched battle. At one point, near Malvern, Pennsylvania, Howe and Washington prepared to do battle, only to have a blind-

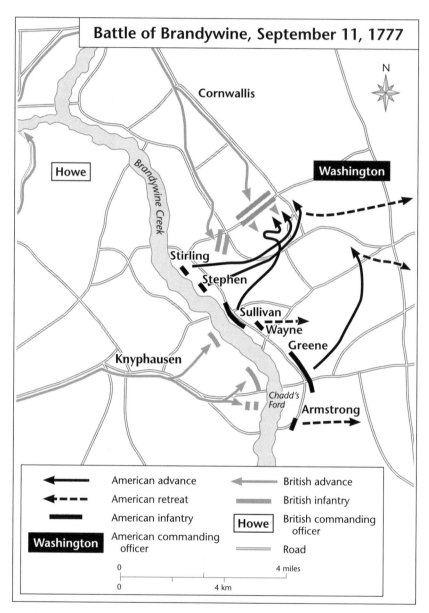

**Battle of Brandywine, September 11, 1777**

N

Cornwallis

Howe

Washington

Brandywine Creek

Stirling

Stephen

Sullivan

Wayne

Greene

Knyphausen

Chadd's Ford

Armstrong

American advance

American retreat

American infantry

Washington — American commanding officer

British advance

British infantry

Howe — British commanding officer

Road

0        4 miles

0        4 km

Washington's defeat at the Battle of Brandywine allowed the British to capture Philadelphia.

## Hessians

To ensure they had sufficient troops to fight the American rebels, the British hired German mercenaries called Hessians. These were professional soldiers who were used in a variety of ways by the British.

ing rainstorm hit. The colonial forces, unable to keep their powder dry, were forced to retreat for more ammunition before the fighting began. On September 23, 1777, as Howe chased Washington around the Pennsylvania countryside, General Lord Charles Cornwallis captured Philadelphia.

The British forces defeated the colonists at the Battle of Brandywine on September 11, 1777. *(Library of Congress, Prints and Photographs Division [LC-USZ62-100726])*

# THE BATTLE OF GERMANTOWN
## October 4, 1777

When the British marched into Philadelphia, the Continental Congress fled to Lancaster, Pennsylvania, and then York, Pennsylvania, both of which can claim to have served as the U.S. capital. With Philadelphia occupied by his troops, General Howe set up his main camp in nearby Germantown. At dawn on October 4, 1777, Washington attacked the British at Germantown and forced them to retreat.

This was the first time, in a pitched battle, that the British soldiers were forced to give ground to the Americans. However, the day was not a complete success. First fog and then miscommunication among the American commanders forced Washington to withdraw from the battle before he lost even more men. Washington believed that if everything had gone according to his battle plan, they might have decisively beaten Howe at Germantown. As it was, the colonials lost more than 1,000 men—killed, wounded, or captured—compared to only 535 casualties for the British.

After Germantown, Howe went about the task of securing his gains. He cleared the Delaware River of traps called chevaux-de-frise that were put in the river to prevent the British from sailing directly to Philadelphia. Howe also had to clear the Patriots out of a number of forts that controlled the river. It took two

## Cheveaux-de-Frise

A cheveaux-de-frise was originally a type of barrier placed in front of forts to prevent mounted soldiers from attacking. During the Revolution, Patriots decided to use something similar to block both the Hudson and Delaware Rivers. The aquatic version of the cheveaux-de-frise was a large wooden crib that was approximately six feet square. Attached to the crib at angles were a number of large logs ranging in length from 30 to 60 feet. The ends of the logs were sheathed in iron that came to a point. The device was floated out into the river, where the crib would be filled with stones from a barge. When a number of these were placed side by side, they created an unseen barrier that would pierce the hull of any ship that was sailed into them.

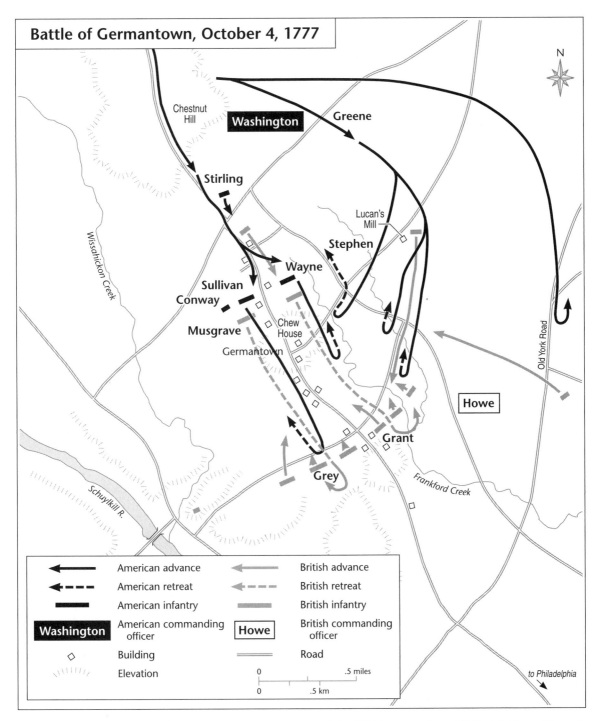

**Battle of Germantown, October 4, 1777**

N

Chestnut Hill

**Washington**

Greene

Stirling

Lucan's Mill

**Stephen**

Wissahickon Creek

Wayne

Sullivan

Conway

Musgrave

Chew House

Germantown

Old York Road

**Howe**

Grant

Schuylkill R.

Frankford Creek

Grey

| | American advance | | British advance |
|---|---|---|---|
| | American retreat | | British retreat |
| | American infantry | | British infantry |
| **Washington** | American commanding officer | **Howe** | British commanding officer |
| ◇ | Building | | Road |
| | Elevation | | |

0     .5 miles

0     .5 km

to Philadelphia

The defeat of the Continental army at Germantown ensured the British possession of Philadelphia and forced Washington and his men to spend a terrible winter at Valley Forge.

separate attacks to capture Fort Mercer at Billingsport, New Jersey. A five-day bombardment from ships in the river was required for the British to gain control of Fort Mifflin, Pennsylvania, but by the

George Washington and his troops spent the winter of 1777–78 at Valley Forge, Pennsylvania, about 20 miles from Philadelphia, which was then occupied by the British. The colonial forces had little food or supplies at their winter camp. On the left of this engraving are Washington and Marie-Joseph-Paul-Yves-Roche-Gilbert du Motier, marquis de Lafayette. *(National Archives/DOD, War & Conflict, #36)*

Pennsylvania

end of November, Howe's forces not only controlled the city of Philadelphia but could now sail directly up the Delaware River with troops and supplies. Secure in Philadelphia, in early December Howe turned his attention once again to Washington's army.

## VALLEY FORGE
## Winter 1777–1778

At the beginning of December 1777, Howe tried to pull off a surprise attack on Washington at Whitemarsh, Pennsylvania. Fortunately, one of Washington's scouts was able to forewarn the general, and he was able to strategically position his troops. On December 8, 1777, Howe probed Washington's flanks with small attacks only to be forced back by the colonial cavalry. Howe decided that Washington was too well positioned to risk a full attack, so he marched his troops back to the comfort of Philadelphia.

Washington moved his forces to Valley Forge on December 19, 1777, where they barely survived the devastating effects of hunger, disease, and brutal winter weather. At Valley Forge, Washington put the troops to work building cabins for themselves. To encourage them to hurry, Washington made the cabin-building a contest with a prize for the first group to finish their cabin. Once the cabins were built, the troops settled in for what turned out to be an extremely severe winter for Pennsylvania.

Shortages of just about everything, including food, clothing, and

## Smallpox Inoculation

For hundreds if not thousands of years, smallpox had been one of the most deadly diseases known to humankind. It devastated the Native American population of North America and killed many colonists. It also raged through Europe with regularity. In the first half of the 18th century it was discovered that people living in the Middle East and Africa were intentionally infected with the disease through a scratch in the skin using the pus from a pox on a sick person. Often, a person infected in this manner would get a very mild form of the disease and then be immune from getting a full-blown, deadly case of smallpox. People in England experimented with the practice and proved that it worked. Dr. Zabdiel Boylston of Boston is credited with introducing the technique into the colonies after experimenting on his own children.

By the time Washington's troops were encamped at Valley Forge, the practice of inoculation had gained wide acceptance. There is no way of knowing how many men, in their weakened condition, would have succumbed to the disease at Valley Forge, but it would likely have been many, many more than 10.

blankets, soon caused great suffering among the troops. Of the 11,000 men who arrived in Valley Forge, 3,000 were soon either too sick or too malnourished to be available for duty. All sorts of problems raged through the camp as the men gambled and fought among themselves. The unsanitary conditions in the crowded camp brought on diseases such as typhoid, typhus, and dysentery. Fortunately, Washington had the foresight to have 4,000 men who had not had smallpox inoculated against the disease in December. In the course of the winter, only 10 people at Valley Forge succumbed to what was one of the deadliest diseases of the time.

A constant problem Washington had to deal with at Valley Forge was desertion. Men regularly walked away from camp and headed home. Those who were caught received a whipping of 100 lashes. In two cases of desertion, Washington went as far as having the offenders hanged. It was not just the troops who suffered at Valley Forge; more than 1,500 horses also died. As spring approached, the situation slowly improved. Food began to arrive regularly, as did other supplies. Baron Frederich Wilhelm von

# Baron Frederick Wilhelm von Steuben
## (1730–1794)

While in Paris in 1777, Benjamin Franklin was introduced to a Prussian army officer who had fought in a number of European wars and had been on Frederick the Great's general staff. Baron Frederick Wilhelm von Steuben was living in Paris on his half-pay pension as a captain. Franklin convinced Steuben to go to America and offer his services to the Continental Congress. Steuben told the Congress that he was a lieutenant general, and he was appointed acting inspector general of the Continental army by George Washington. Steuben is credited with reorganizing Washington's army and teaching the troops at Valley Forge the discipline that made European armies more efficient fighting forces. In addition to drilling the soldiers at Valley Forge, Steuben wrote the army's first manual of procedures.

After George Washington agreed to his plan, Baron Frederick Wilhelm von Steuben helped train the Continental army at Valley Forge. In this engraving of various Revolutionary War officers, Washington is on the far left and von Steuben is the third from the left. *(Library of Congress, Prints and Photographs Division [LC-USZ62-67559])*

Steuben joined Washington at the end of February 1778, which had a positive effect on the entire army.

Steuben fashioned Washington's ragtag army into a much more disciplined and effective fighting force. The soldiers gained confidence from his instruction. The troops that marched out of Valley Forge on June 19, 1778, were much more prepared to fight the British than were those that had been defeated at Brandywine and lost their advantage in the confusion of Germantown. As Steuben worked his magic at Valley Forge, Benjamin Franklin was working his own in Paris.

## FRENCH ALLIES

The Continental Congress sent Benjamin Franklin to France in 1777 in the hope that he could negotiate a treaty between the Patriot government in North America and the French in Paris. The French had already aided the Patriots by supplying them with military supplies starting in May 1776. However, if the Americans were going to defeat the British, they needed more than just supplies. When news reached Paris of an American victory at Saratoga, New York, on October 17, 1777, the French decided it was time to join the Americans.

The French were afraid that if the war started going in favor of the Americans, the British would try to reconcile with their rebellious colonies. On February 6, 1778, Charles Gravier, comte de Vergennes, the French foreign minister, signed two treaties, one of which provided the direct help that Franklin sought. Vergennes agreed to officially recognize the United States and to supply them with direct military aid. A French fleet was sent to protect the American coast, and a large number of French soldiers joined Washington. The addition of the French into the Revolutionary War helped turn the tide in the Patriots' favor and forced the British leaders in North America to rethink their plans.

## THE EVACUATION OF PHILADELPHIA

In February 1778, General Sir William Howe resigned his command and was succeeded by General Sir Henry Clinton. General Clinton decided that it was time to turn his attention to the south and decided to give up Philadelphia. The thinking was that in the far southern colonies of Georgia and South Carolina there was a large Loyalist population waiting to assist the British. Once the far South was in British hands, they could work their way through North Carolina and into Virginia, which seemed, like Massachusetts, to be a hotbed of the Revolution.

Before General Clinton could send an army to the South, he had to concentrate his northern forces in the British stronghold of New York City. This meant giving Philadelphia back to the Patriots. The main force of his army marched across New Jersey and was almost caught by Washington at Monmouth, New Jersey, on June 27, 1778. Some 3,000 Loyalists sailed away from Philadelphia with General Clinton. Many of the Loyalists probably feared Patriot reprisals without the protection of a British force in the city.

The Continental Congress moved back to Philadelphia and remained there for a number of years. Clinton and his second in command, General Lord Cornwallis experienced numerous successes in the South until Washington and the French surrounded Cornwallis at Yorktown, Virginia, and he was forced to surrender on October 17, 1781.

When the Revolutionary War began in 1775, Charles, Lord Cornwallis volunteered to serve. This image shows him much later in life. *(National Archives, Still Picture Records [NWDNS-148-GW-463])*

## WAR ON THE FRONTIER

Although both the American and British armies left Pennsylvania in summer 1778, the area around Philadelphia was not the only battleground. Along the frontier, Loyalist forces allied themselves with Indians as the French had done and raided all along the Pennsylvania frontier. The worst of these raids is known as the Wyoming Valley Massacre.

Major Sir John Butler led a force that consisted of 1,200 Loyalist militia and their Native American allies. Along the Susquehanna River near Pittston, which is halfway between Wilkes-Barre and Scranton, were two forts—Forty Fort and Fort Wintermot. After Butler and his men captured Fort Wintermot, they attacked Forty Fort and were unsuccessful at first. Butler then made it look like he was leaving the area by setting Fort Wintermot on fire and heading out into the forest. However, many of his men waited, hoping to ambush the defenders of Forty Fort when they came out to investigate.

The Patriots took the bait, and a large number of them were killed or captured. The Native Americans tied some of the captives to trees and then set them on fire. This sort of fighting between Loyalists and Patriots, who in some instances used to be neighbors, happened throughout the Revolution. When the war finally came to an end at Yorktown, there were many reprisals against people who were known or thought to have been Loyalists. Many other Loyalists packed up and left for Canada and England after the war. All those who stayed behind were faced with the challenge of creating states and a country from what they had won from Britain in the Revolution.

# 9

# Becoming Part
# of a Nation

## SHAPING PENNSYLVANIA

If Pennsylvania had been held within the bounds of Penn's original charter, it would have been about half the size it is today. During the 18th century, the original land of Pennsylvania was expanded by a number of purchases from Native Americans and by settling conflicting claims with Virginia, Maryland, and Connecticut.

The conflict with Maryland was settled by the English courts in 1750, but it took more than a decade for the descendants of the two original proprietors, William Penn and Lord Baltimore, to agree on the settlement. In 1763, two surveyors from England, Charles Mason and Jeremiah Dixon, arrived in Philadelphia. Their first task was to set the north-south line dividing what would become Delaware and Maryland. Once they established that, they began to determine the east-west line between Pennsylvania and Maryland. It took the two surveyors and their helpers almost four years to complete the survey of the 233-mile-long border between the two colonies.

After settling its boundary issues, Pennsylvania still had to deal with claims by two other colonies. Connecticut was one of the colonies that originally had an Atlantic-to-Pacific-Ocean land grant. Since the Dutch settled immediately to the west and that land then became part of New York, little was done about the western claims of Connecticut until 1753. People in Connecticut

# The Mason-Dixon Line

The names of the two surveyors who set the boundary between Pennsylvania and Maryland might have been lost to history except for a major event in the history of the United States. When the argument between the North and South over the admission of new states reached an impasse over where slavery would be allowed, the Missouri Compromise of 1820 used the east-west portion of the Mason-Dixon Line as the dividing line between the slave states of the South and the free states of the North. Some believe the nickname, "Dixie," for the South may have been derived from the name of the line that divided it from the North.

Charles Mason and Jeremiah Dixon established the boundary between Pennsylvania and Maryland that later became known as the Mason-Dixon Line. This stone marker, covered by the emblems of the two states it separates, was erected between 1763 and 1767. *(Library of Congress, Prints and Photographs Division [HABS, PA,1-ZORA.V,1-1])*

formed the Susquehanna Company with the intention of moving settlers into an area that is now the northeast corner of Pennsylvania. The government in London told officials in Connecticut that they could not settle the area without permission from the Crown. It was not until 1773 that Connecticut received the go-ahead to claim land along the Susquehanna River.

These settlements created instant conflict with Pennsylvanians already in the area. Some of the Connecticut settlers were killed during the Wyoming Valley Massacre in 1778 and many more went back into Connecticut seeking safety. When the Revolutionary War ended, some of the Connecticut settlers moved back into the disputed land area. Others never left. Connecticut and Pennsylvania turned to the Continental Congress in 1786 to settle their land dispute. Connecticut's "land grab" had been on shaky ground from the very beginning. A commission appointed by the congress took Pennsylvania's side, and Connecticut gave up its claim.

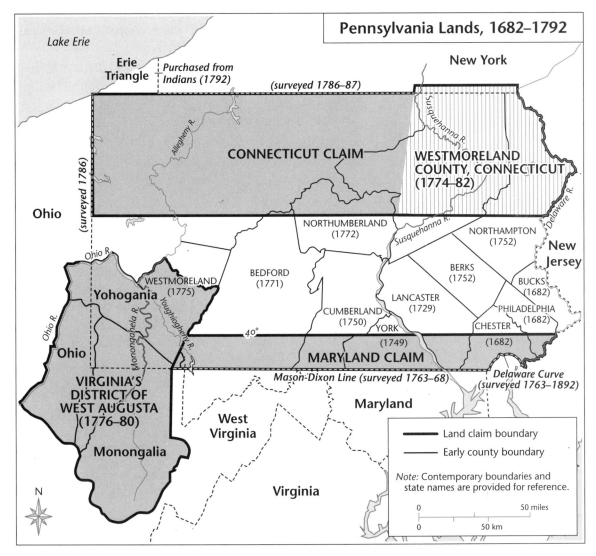

Maryland, Virginia, Connecticut, and a number of Native American tribes laid claim to sections of land that eventually became part of Pennsylvania.

Pennsylvania had to deal with another attempt to take a section of the state. Land companies from Virginia tried to acquire land in the southwest corner of the state. Virginia aggressively sought to expand westward throughout the colonial period, and it was not until it was forced to compromise with the other states to get the Articles of Confederation ratified that it gave up most of its claim. At the beginning of the Revolution, three different land companies claimed parts of Pennsylvania in what was called the District of West Augusta. In 1779, Virginia gave up its land claims north of the Mason-Dixon line. Then, in 1784, the western boundary of Pennsylvania was surveyed.

Throughout the colonial period, Pennsylvania's official policy was to pay Native Americans for any lands that were opened to settlers. At times, settlers would get to unsettled areas before the government had negotiated for the land and conflicts would ensue. In 1791, Pennsylvania bought its final piece of land from the Iroquois. This section of land along Lake Erie, known as the Erie Triangle, gave the state access to the Great Lakes and, much later, to the Erie Canal and the Saint Lawrence Seaway.

## THE STATE CONSTITUTION

As soon as the thirteen colonies declared independence, the Patriot leaders in Pennsylvania set about writing a new state constitution. This turned out to be the most democratic of any of the original state constitutions, and it created almost as many problems as it solved when it was adopted on September 28, 1776. The new Pennsylvania constitution granted much more power to the people. It called for a large assembly that solved the problem that existed where the eastern part of the colony had held a disproportionate number of seats in the colonial assembly. It also expanded the right to vote. Most colonies, before and after the Revolution, had property requirements for voters. The new Pennsylvania constitution awarded voting rights as follows:

> Every freemen of the full age of twenty-one Years, having resided in this state for the space of one whole Year next before the day of election for representatives, and paid public taxes during that time, shall enjoy the right of an elector: Provided always,

In this painting, colonists raise the first U.S. flag over Independence Hall in Philadelphia. *(National Archives/DOD, War & Conflict, #23)*

# The Abolition of Slavery

The Germantown Resolution of 1688 had expressed the feelings of many in Pennsylvania about slavery. Most of the people in the colony and then the state were opposed to it. In 1775, Benjamin Franklin, Thomas Paine, Benjamin Rush, and a number of others formed a group that came to be known as the Pennsylvania Abolition Society to work toward putting an end to slavery. Slavery was a hotly debated topic during the Revolution and the Constitutional Convention because many felt that when the Declaration of Independence stated "that all men are created equal," it should apply to African-American slaves as well. In 1780, Pennsylvania became the first state to begin the process of abolishing slavery. By 1800, only 55 of the 6,500 African Americans in Philadelphia remained in slavery.

Benjamin Franklin opposed slavery and helped form the Pennsylvania Abolition Society. *(National Archives/DOD, War & Conflict, #65)*

The Pennsylvania Assembly passed the Act for the Gradual Abolition of Slavery in 1780. The first law of its kind, the act called for the freeing of all slaves in Pennsylvania born after the act's passage once they reached age 28. *(Pennsylvania State Archives)*

that sons of freeholders of the age of twenty-one years shall be entitled to vote although they have not paid taxes.

This constitution also allowed African-American taxpayers to vote.

Despite liberal voting rights, a large percentage of the people in Pennsylvania were excluded from voting by another provision of the state constitution. The writers of the constitution, who were led by Benjamin Franklin, included a loyalty oath. This created a real problem for the Quakers of Pennsylvania who felt that their religious beliefs made it wrong for them to swear any oaths. Many Quakers refused to swear the new oath and were thus left out of the political process. As much as the new constitution was a cause for concern for Pennsylvania, another document, the Articles of Confederation, adopted by the Continental Congress in 1776, created problems for the struggling federal government.

## ARTICLES OF CONFEDERATION

The Second Continental Congress was able to raise an army and direct the war efforts of the United States, but it had no real authority. In June 1776, the congress created a committee to come up with a plan for a federal government. John Dickinson of Pennsylvania chaired the committee that came up with a plan for a fairly strong central government. When the plan was presented to the congress, it quickly became apparent that many of the delegates would not support it.

Each colony had come about through an almost unique set of circumstances, and the people identified with their respective colonies. People in Pennsylvania were loyal to their state and had no sense of a national identity. The same was true in most of the colonies. As a compromise, the Articles of Confederation were drawn up and sent to the states in 1777 for approval. All the states had to agree for the articles to become the law of the land.

A number of problems arose during the ratification process. One of the problems had to do with the lands to the west of the Appalachian Mountains. Some states, among them the Carolinas, Virginia, and New York, claimed lands to the west. When New York and Virginia agreed to give up their claims to western lands to the federal government, Maryland finally became the last state to ratify the Articles of Confederation in 1781.

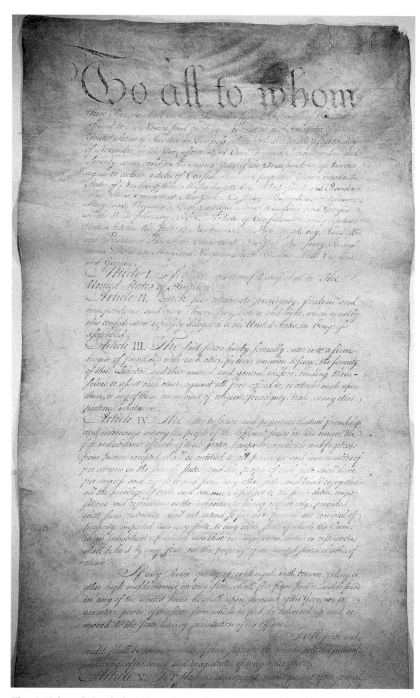

The Articles of Confederation, shown here, were written by a committee of the Continental Congress and intended as a constitution for the colonies. *(National Archives, National Archives Building, NWCTB-360-MISC-ROLL10F81)*

By the time the Treaty of Paris, which settled many of the differences between the new United States and Britain, was finally signed in 1783, more problems had developed with the Articles of Confederation. The federal government was having trouble paying its debts. It had no source of income and had to ask the states for money. Most states gave the federal government only a small portion of what was needed to meet the government's obligations. As a result, some of the soldiers who served in the Revolution did not receive their full pay.

In summer 1783, approximately 100 soldiers marched on the hall where the Continental Congress was in session in Philadelphia. These soldiers demanded their back pay. However, the congress had no money. Rather than deal with the soldiers, the congress moved their meetings to Princeton, New Jersey.

Although many in Pennsylvania continued to prosper after the Revolution, many of the other states experienced economic hard times as the former colonies adjusted to their new status as part of an independent country. Personal debt was soon as big a problem as public debt. Those who had borrowed heavily to rebuild their farms and plantations after the war were having trouble repaying their loans. After the war, there was a general depression in the economy throughout the new United States. In Massachusetts, in 1786 and 1787, a group of farmers protested against problems caused by mounting debt. This has come to be known as Shays's Rebellion. There was no organized rebellion in Pennsylvania, but some of the people in the state experienced hard times.

By 1786, a number of problems between the states had developed and some of the states sent representatives to a convention in Annapolis, Maryland. The intent of the Annapolis Convention was to consider a federal plan to regulate trade. Only five states—Virginia, Delaware, New York, Pennsylvania, and New Jersey—sent delegates. The delegates quickly realized that they had two problems. One was the lack of attendance by the other states, and the other was the limitations of the Articles of Confederation.

The delegates to the Annapolis Convention, led by Alexander Hamilton, sent out a call for a convention the following year in Philadelphia. The idea of the convention was to amend the Articles of Confederation to solve some of the problems being faced by the states.

# THE CONSTITUTIONAL CONVENTION
## 1787

When the delegates convened in Philadelphia in May 1787, they quickly decided that the Articles of Confederation needed to be scrapped and a new document organizing the federal government drawn up. Not only were there problems with the articles themselves, but it also required all 13 states to agree to make any amendments—and only 12 states sent delegates. The smallest state, Rhode Island, which feared losing its independence in a federal system, refused to participate in the Constitutional Convention. The list of delegates who did come to Philadelphia included many well-known Patriot leaders. George Washington was elected to serve as president of the convention.

There were many controversies surrounding the writing of the Constitution. The delegates had to compromise on many issues and balance the desire of the states to control their own affairs and the

The Constitutional Convention convened in Philadelphia in May 1787 and remained in session until mid-September. *(Library of Congress, Prints and Photographs Division [LC-USZ62-92869])*

## The Pennsylvania Delegation to the Constitutional Convention
### 1787

When the Constitutional Convention opened in Philadelphia in May 1787, Pennsylvania sent eight men to represent the state. They were:

Benjamin Franklin        Thomas Fitzsimons
Thomas Mifflin           Jared Ingersoll
Robert Morris            James Wilson
George Clymer            Gouverneur Morris

Gouverneur Morris represented Pennsylvania at the Constitutional Convention. *(Library of Congress, Prints and Photographs Division [LC-USZ62-107076])*

need for a federal government to unite and lead the country. One major hurdle was the way the states would be represented in the national congress. The large states, like Massachusetts and Virginia, wanted representation to be based on population. The small states wanted every state to have equal representation. Eventually, what is known as the Great Compromise was reached.

The Great Compromise created the U.S. Senate, which would have equal representation from each state, and the U.S. House of Representatives, in which states would have a varying number of representatives based on population. This compromise has worked well for more than 200 years.

Once those attending the convention had agreed on the Constitution, they had to send it to the states to be ratified. They determined that the Constitution would go into effect when nine states

## Preamble to the U.S. Constitution

*We the People of the United States, in Order to form a more perfect Union, establish Justice, insure domestic Tranquility, provide for the common defence, promote the general Welfare, and secure the Blessings of Liberty to ourselves and our Posterity, do ordain and establish this Constitution for the United States of America.*

had ratified it. Delaware, which had been a part of Pennsylvania for many years, was the first to ratify the constitution, on December 7, 1787. Just five days later, the Pennsylvania assembly voted to ratify the new U.S. Constitution, and Pennsylvania became the second state, on December 12, 1787. However, the Constitution did not go into effect until June 1788, when New Hampshire became the ninth state to ratify the Constitution. Rhode Island, which had stayed out of the Constitutional Convention, became the last state to ratify on May 29, 1790. Thus, Pennsylvania, which had been the setting for so many of the Patriots' meetings, was now truly a part of the United States.

# Pennsylvania
# Time Line

## 1608

★ Captain John Smith sails up the Susquehanna River from Virginia, visiting the Susquehannock and giving the English a claim to the area.

## 1609

★ Henry Hudson sails his ship, the *Half Moon*, into Delaware Bay, claiming the land for the Dutch.

## 1610

★ Captain Samuel Argall from Virginia sails into Delaware Bay, claiming it for Virginia governor Lord de la Warr.

## 1615

★ The French explorer Étienne Brulé scouts Pennsylvania.

## 1616

★ The Dutch explorer Cornelius Hendrickson scouts the Delaware region.

## 1623

★ Dutch navigator Cornelius Jacobsen visits the Delaware region.

## 1643

★ Swedes under Governor Johan Printz of New Sweden establish the first permanent settlement in Pennsylvania on Tinicum Island.

## 1655

★ New Netherland governor Peter Stuyvesant seizes New Sweden.

## 1664

★ The British take control of New Netherland, which leads to Pennsylvania, New Jersey, and Delaware becoming colonies.

## 1675

★ Quakers hold their first meeting at Upland, now Chester, Pennsylvania.

## 1681

★ Pennsylvania is given as a royal grant to William Penn. Penn wants a haven for members of the Society of Friends (Quakers) who were being persecuted in England.
★ **April:** Penn sends William Markham, his cousin, to the colony, naming him deputy governor.
★ Penn writes the First Frame of Government.

## 1682

★ King Charles II gives three counties to Penn. These counties now comprise Delaware.
★ Philadelphia is laid out.
★ **October:** Penn arrives in Pennsylvania, sailing on the *Welcome*; he creates the first three counties.
★ **December 4:** The First General Assembly meets with Penn in Chester, and Delaware and Pennsylvania are joined.
★ **December 7:** The General Assembly adopts the First Frame, which forms the basis of law in Pennsylvania.

## 1683

★ The Second Assembly meets, amending Penn's First Frame, and writes the Second Frame of Government.

## 1684

★ William Penn leaves Pennsylvania for England.

## 1688

★ The Quakers publicly voice their opposition to slavery.
★ Due to the English Revolution of 1688 and the overthrow of James II, Penn is deprived of his grant from 1692 to 1694.

## 1696

★ David Lloyd demands more power for the assembly, which is granted in Markham's Frame of Government.

## 1699

★ **December:** Penn comes back to Pennsylvania, staying until 1701.

## 1701

★ Before his return to England, Penn and the assembly agree on a new constitution.

## 1717

★ Scots-Irish immigrants start their migration to Pennsylvania, settling in the Cumberland Valley, then moving farther into western and central Pennsylvania; people from Scotland make up one-quarter of the population of Pennsylvania by the American Revolution.

## 1723

★ Benjamin Franklin first reaches Philadelphia.

## 1727

★ German immigrants increasingly move to the area, mostly settling in interior in Berks, Lancaster, Lehigh, Northampton counties.

## 1730

★ Some 4,000 African slaves are brought to Pennsylvania, although Quakers oppose slavery.

## 1737

★ The Walking Purchase occurs, in which Pennsylvania receives land from the Lenni Lenape and Shawnee.

## 1740

★ An academy is started that will become the College of Philadelphia in 1755 and later the University of Pennsylvania, the only nondenominational college in the colonies.

## until 1753

★ The assembly is dominated by the Quakers.

## 1753

★ Governor Lord Robert Dinwiddie sends George Washington to deliver a letter to the French commander of Fort Le Boeuf (Waterford) asking why the French are invading British territory. This triggers the French and Indian wars in Pennsylvania.

## 1753–54

★ France attempts to control the upper Ohio Valley with forts at Erie (Fort Presque Isle), Waterford (Fort Le Boeuf), Pittsburgh (Fort Duquesne), and Franklin (Fort Machault).

## 1754

★ Colonel George Washington is defeated at Fort Necessity, the first battle of the French and Indian wars in Pennsylvania.

## 1755

★ General Edward Braddock's British and American troops are slaughtered at Monongahela.

## 1758

★ General John Forbes recaptures Pittsburgh.

## 1763

★ As part of Pontiac's War, the Lenni Lenape, Shawnee, and western Seneca attack and destroy Fort LeBoeuf (Waterford), Venango, and Presque Isle (Erie).

★ After 1763, members of the Penn family, who were no longer Quakers, served as governors and often found themselves at odds with the Quaker majority in the Assembly.

★ **June:** Lenni Lenape, Shawnee, and western Seneca begin a siege of Fort Pitt at present-day Pittsburgh.

★ **August 5:** Battle of Bushy Run—Colonel Henry Bouquet, on his way to Fort Pitt, is attacked by the Lenni Lenape, Mingo, Shawnee, and Wyandot.

★ **August 6:** Bouquet defeats the Indian attackers.

## 1764

★ Chief Pontiac is defeated out west.

## 1765

★ Philadelphia is a center of protest over the Stamp Act.

## 1767

★ The Townshend Duties are passed in Parliament, putting taxes on glass, tea, paper, and other imported products. There are protests in Pennsylvania: John Dickinson, a Philadelphia lawyer, writes 12 essays saying Parliament has no right to tax colonists who boycott British products.

## 1770

★ The Townshend Duties are repealed except the tax on tea.

## 1773

★ By 1773, there are now 11 counties, eight more than the original three.

★ John Penn is both a proprietor and governor of the colony.

★ The Tea Act is passed by Parliament. Philadelphians say they will tar and feather the captain of the British ship *Polly*, which returns to Britain without unloading its cargo.

## 1774

★ Philadelphia supports Boston in its protest of the Intolerable Acts.
★ **fall:** Philadelphia hosts the First Continental Congress, which meets to discuss the British retaliation against Massachusetts after the Boston Tea Party. The congress chooses Philadelphian John Dickinson, a moderate who does not want independence from Britain, to write the protest.

## 1775

★ **May 10:** The Second Continental Congress convenes in Philadelphia. Benjamin Franklin, recently returned from Britain as Pennsylvania's agent, is a delegate.
★ **August:** Pennsylvania sends a rifle battalion to defend Boston during the siege.

## 1776

★ By 1776, stagecoach lines run from Philadelphia to southcentral Pennsylvania. Philadelphia has become an important trade center for the colonies and beyond.
★ Pennsylvania has troops in Canadian, New York, and New Jersey battles.
★ During the American Revolution, Pennsylvania farmers supply food for the Patriots. At Carlisle, Pennsylvania, the ordnance arsenal makes cannons, muskets, pikes, and swords.
★ **June:** Pennsylvania's radicals instruct their delegates to vote for independence. Struggles between the Assembly and the Patriots lead to the creation of committees, which call for a state convention.
★ **July 4:** The Declaration of Independence is signed at the Continental Congress in Philadelphia.

★ **July 15:** The convention meets and establishes the Council of Safety to rule instead of the assembly.

★ **September 28:** The convention adopts a new constitution, with an assembly of one house and executive council, as well as a Declaration of Rights, which is still in use. It is opposed by John Dickinson, Robert Morris, Frederick Muhlenberg, and James Wilson. The Patriots remain in power until 1790.

★ **December:** General George Washington sets up headquarters on the western bank of the Delaware River after his defeat in New Jersey.

★ **December 26:** Washington's troops recross the Delaware, defeating the British at Trenton, New Jersey.

## 1777

★ **September 11:** The Battle of Brandywine is fought near Chadd's Ford, 25 miles south of Philadelphia. General Sir William Howe, commander of all British troops in America, positions his 18,000 troops against General Washington's 11,000 troops. The Patriots are forced to retreat to Chester. However, the American troops prevent the British under Howe from reaching Philadelphia until September 26.

★ The Continental Congress flees Philadelphia for Lancaster, then York, until June 27, 1778.

★ **September 26:** British troops under General Lord Charles Cornwallis capture Philadelphia.

★ **October 4:** The Battle of Germantown is fought. General Washington begins a surprise attack at dawn in fog against British troops at Germantown, five miles outside Philadelphia. The Americans retreat, but people are encouraged that Washington was quick to go back into battle after the Battle of Brandywine.

## 1777–78

★ British troops occupy Philadelphia.

★ **December 1777–June 1778:** Washington and his troops spend the winter at Valley Forge.

- ★ **spring 1778:** The British begin to leave Philadelphia, in part because of the French coming in on the side of the Patriots. The Continental Congress returns to Philadelphia.
- ★ **July:** As part of a series of skirmishes, Loyalists and Native Americans attack the frontier settlements; attacks are bloodiest at Wyoming in July.

## 1779

- ★ John Sullivan and Daniel Brodhead lead expeditions in western Pennsylvania against the British and the Six Nations of the Iroquois.
- ★ The assembly passes a law that gives the Penn family some compensation and takes the family's remaining land in Pennsylvania.

## 1780

- ★ By 1780, Pennsylvania had given $16 million to Congress; 90 Philadelphians loaned £300,000 to supply the army.
- ★ Pennsylvania passes the Pennsylvania Gradual Abolition Act, outlawing slavery. It is the first state to do so.

## 1784

- ★ Pennsylvania buys land claimed by the Six Nations. It will buy more in 1789.

## 1785

- ★ Pennsylvania buys out the Lenni Lenape and Wyandot land claims. The tribes move west.

## 1787

- ★ The federal Constitutional Convention meets in Philadelphia because the Articles of Confederation are not holding the colonies together and the federal government is in dire financial shape. Benjamin Franklin, Gouverneur Morris, and James Wilson sign the U.S. Constitution in Philadelphia on September 17.

- ★ **November 21:** In Philadelphia, the Pennsylvania Assembly is called together by conservatives. However, Federalists, led by Wilson, elect the majority of delegates.
- ★ **December 12:** Pennsylvania ratifies the U.S. Constitution, the second state to do so.

## 1790

- ★ According to the 1790 census, of 10,000 African Americans in Pennsylvania, about 6,300 had been freed.

# Pennsylvania Historical Sites

## BIRDSBORO

**Daniel Boone Homestead**    Daniel Boone, who became famous for settling the lands west of the Appalachian Mountains, was born on this homestead in 1734 and lived here for the first 10 years of his life. The homestead includes 579 acres with numerous historic buildings.

> *Address:* 400 Daniel Boone Road, Birdsboro, Pennsylvania
>    19508
> *Phone:* 610-582-4900
> *Web Site:* www.danielboonehomestead.org

## CHADDS FORD

**Brandywine Battlefield Park**    On September 11, 1777, George Washington's troops fought the British under General Sir William Howe at the Battle of Brandywine. Today, a visitor's center with a museum commemorates the battle. Tours of Washington and Lafayette's headquarters are available.

> *Address:* Box 202, Chadds Ford, Pennsylvania 19317
> *Phone:* 610-459-3342
> *Web Site:* www.ushistory.org/brandywine

# CORNWALL

**Cornwall Iron Furnace**   The Cornwall Iron Furnace was in operation from 1742 until 1883. It made cannon barrels that were used during the Revolution.

> *Address:* P.O. Box 251, Cornwall, Pennsylvania 17016
> *Phone:* 717-272-9711
> *Web Site:* www.phmc.state.pa.us/bhsm/toh/cornwall/
> cornwalliron.asp?secid=14

# EPHRATA

**Ephrata Cloister**   This place of religious seclusion was started in 1732 by German immigrants and is now open to the public.

> *Address:* 632 West Main Street, Ephrata, Pennsylvania 17522
> *Phone:* 717-733-6600, ext. 3001
> *Web Site:* www.ephratacloister.org

# FORT WASHINGTON

**Hope Lodge Historic Site**   One of the best examples of Georgian architecture (a style popular during the reigns of Georges I, II, and III in England) in Pennsylvania, Hope Lodge was built by Quaker merchant Samuel Morris between 1743 and 1748.

> *Address:* 553 South Bethlehem Pike, Fort Washington,
> Pennsylvania 19034
> *Phone:* 215-646-1595
> *Web Site:* www.ushistory.org/hope

# HORSHAM

**Graeme Park**   Graeme Park is the site of the Keith House, the only remaining house of a colonial Pennsylvania governor.

> *Address:* 859 County Line Road, Horsham, Pennsylvania
> 19044

Phone: 215-343-0965
Web Site: www.ushistory.org/graeme

## JEANNETTE

**Bushy Run Battlefield**   The Bushy Run Battlefield visitor center commemorates the battle where Colonel Henry Bouquet's forces defeated the Native Americans on August 5 and 6, 1763.

Address: Route 993, Jeannette, Pennsylvania 15644
Phone: 724-627-5584
Web Site: www.bushyrunbattlefield.com

## LANCASTER

**Landis Valley Museum**   A "living history" museum, the Landis Valley Museum portrays life among the Pennsylvania Germans from 1740 through 1940.

Address: 2451 Kissel Hill Road, Lancaster, Pennsylvania 17001
Phone: 717-569-0401
Web Site: www.landisvalleymuseum.org

## MORRISVILLE

**Pennsbury Manor**   The country house of William Penn in Bucks County has been recreated and is open to the public.

Address: 400 Pennsbury Memorial Road, Morrisville,
    Pennsylvania 19067
Phone: 215-946-0400
Web Site: www.pennsburymanor.org

## PHILADELPHIA

**Independence National Historical Park**   Independence National Historical Park includes the Independence Visitor Center, Independence Hall Museum, and the Liberty Bell Center Museum.

**Address:** 143 South Third Street, Philadelphia, Pennsylvania
19106
**Phone:** 215-597-8974
**Web Site:** www.nps.gov/inde

# PITTSBURGH

**Fort Pitt**   The Fort Pitt Museum's exhibits focus on the history and significance of Fort Pitt during the French and Indian wars.

**Address:** 101 Commonwealth, Point State Park, Pittsburgh,
Pennsylvania 15222
**Phone:** 412-281-9284
**Web Site:** www.fortpittmuseum.com

# PROSPECT PARK

**Morton Homestead**   The Morton Homestead is an 18th-century Swedish log house that was lived in by John Morton, one of the signers of the Declaration of Independence.

**Address:** 100 Lincoln Avenue, Prospect Park, Pennsylvania 19076
**Phone:** 610-583-7221
**Web Site:** www.phmc.state.pa.us/bhsm/toh/morton/
mortonhomestead.asp?secid=14

# SOMERSET

**Somerset Historical Center**   The Somerset Historical Center is a 14-acre rural history museum that features a 1773 farmstead with a log settler's cabin as well as a historical center.

**Address:** 10649 Somerset Pike, Somerset, Pennsylvania 15501
**Phone:** 814-445-6077
**Web Site:** www.somersethistoricalcenter.org

# WASHINGTON CROSSING

**Washington Crossing Historic Park**   The 500-acre site where General George Washington and his troops crossed the Delaware

River includes 13 historic buildings and the 100-acre Bowman's Hill Wildflower Preserve.

*Address:* P.O. Box 103, Washington Crossing, Pennsylvania 18977

*Phone:* 215-493-4076

*Web Site:* www.phmc.state.pa.us/bhsm/toh/washington/ washingtoncrossing.asp?secid=14

## WOMELSDORF

**Conrad Weiser Homestead**    Weiser is famous for being Pennsylvania's ambassador to the Iroquois. His stone house, its outbuildings, and grounds are open to the public.

*Address:* 28 Weiser Road, Womelsdorf, Pennsylvania 19567

*Phone:* 610-589-2934

*Web Site:* www.phmc.state.pa.us/bhsm/toh/weiser/ conradweiser.asp?secid=14

# Further Reading

## BOOKS

Fradin, Dennis B. *The Pennsylvania Colony*. Chicago: Children's Press, 1988.

Illick, Joseph E. *Colonial Pennsylvania: A History*. New York: Scribner's, 1976.

Italia, Bob. *The Pennsylvania Colony*. Edina, Minn.: ABDO Publishing, 2001.

Kelley, Joseph J. *Pennsylvania: The Colonial Years, 1681–1776*. New York: Doubleday, 1980.

Miller, Randall M., and William Pencak, eds. *Pennsylvania: A History of the Commonwealth*. University Park: Pennsylvania State University Press, 2002.

Sherrow, Victoria. *Pennsylvania*. San Diego: Lucent Books, 2002.

## WEB SITES

Pennsylvania Historical and Museum Commission. "Outline of Pennsylvania History." Available online. URL: www.phmc. state.pa.us/bah/pahist/pahistoutline.asp?secid=31. Downloaded March 2, 2004.

Pennsylvania Historical and Museum Commission. "Pennsylvania State History: The Quaker Province: 1681–1776." Available online. URL: www.phmc.state.pa.us/bah/pahist/quaker.asp? secid=31. Downloaded March 2, 2004.

Pennsylvania Historical and Museum Commission. "Pennsylvania Trail of History." Available online. URL: www.phmc.state.pa.us/bhsm/trailofhistory.asp?secid=14. Downloaded March 2, 2004.

Smith, Larry D. "Mother Bedford." (A site devoted to the history of Old Bedford County, Pennsylvania.) Available online. URL: www.motherbedford.com. Downloaded March 2, 2004.

# Index

Page numbers in *italic* indicate photographs. Page numbers in **boldface** indicate box features. Page numbers followed by m indicate maps. Page numbers followed by c indicate time line entries. Page numbers followed by t indicate a table or graph.